How to Build a Healthy Financial Future

Build a Healthy Financial Future

Lessons Learned as an Economist and Bankruptcy Attorney

Stephen M. Enderton

ISBN:978-1-7376710-3-9
Marble Dog Publishing, LLC
Salt Lake City, Utah

DEDICATION

"To my wife who edited this book. Without her help as a professional writer and loving wife I would be lost.

To my children who have put up with me during a long working career without complaint.

To my economics and law professors who gave me the knowledge to understand what I have seen through my client's lives.

To my many clients who gave me the insight to write this book.

Choose a job you love and you will never have to work a day in your life.

Confucius

TABLE OF CONTENTS

Introduction

My name is Stephen Enderton. I earned an economics degree from the University of Utah and a law degree from the University of Denver, Strum College of Law. As an economist I naturally had an interest in an area of law that focused on economics. My practice specialized in bankruptcy law, debt negotiation and credit repair; all of those are related to economics. Interestingly, this was not an area I chose. My first few years as an attorney I was in general practice where I handled divorce, personal injury, debt collection, criminal law, and dabbled in bankruptcy law. I helped set-up business entities, provided advice relating to operating a business; I had clients who were just starting out with an abundance of hope, and those who were at their worst.

The ones at their worst often had a difficult time abandoning misplaced ideas that I was sure led to their failures. Such ideas can lead to a business failure, bankruptcy or even to committing crime out of frustration when the situation is extreme. While I always attempted to help, not all clients accepted sound advice.

Ultimately, I landed primarily in bankruptcy law and closely related areas. I have seen people in almost every kind of financial distress, not only those who had business failures, but also those who had lost jobs, had catastrophic medical bills, and several who were just plain poor money managers.

This book primarily addresses issues relating to creating a sound financial future and ways to avoid financial distress. While not all situations can be avoided there are basic principles and ideas in this book that can be implemented to minimize the chance of ever having traumatic financial distress. While it is not always possible to avoid distress, it is possible to be prepared to weather most stressful situations. While each situation is different, the one common thread is that better planning and preparation will help. Can all catastrophic financial situations be averted? Of course not, but many can either be avoided or the severity can be diminished.

While I worked for many years helping people get a fresh start through bankruptcy, it just doesn't seem like it was enough. Unfortunately, some clients returned to file another bankruptcy. Often when a case is successfully completed, I tell clients I love seeing them but that for their sake, I hope to never see them again. I found that much of my work was teaching clients new ideas and habits so they could avoid bankruptcy in the future. Some learned, some did not. Hopefully, you will find sound financial advice to foster habits that help you avoid financial distress, and in the event you have already filed a bankruptcy, this book will help you repair your credit so you can return to financial stability.

My experience has taught me the principles that will help you stay financially vibrant.

Just about everyone has an opinion about how to have a lucrative financial future. Some simply say that you don't need to build credit because you should just stay out of debt. Frankly, that is simplistic and not very realistic. It is virtually impossible to function in modern society without some credit. Most people want to buy a nice home and drive a nice car; these require credit.

This book will give you some ideas on how you can maintain and rejuvenate your financial future and build your credit.

Chapter 1

Basics Everybody Should Know

Our greatest glory
is not in never falling,
but in rising every time we fall.
Confucius

The place to start is long before you get into trouble. Many people get into trouble because they simply do not trust anybody else so they muddle through their finances on their own. No matter the educational background ranging from not having a formal education to having a graduate degree, it is not possible for anyone to understand everything. Most doctors know better than to attempt to rewire a home on their own and most electricians know they cannot fix their own hernias. It is just a fact we can't specialize in everything. Does that mean we simply take somebody else's opinion as to what to do? No, of course not. But it should mean we at least seek good advice. Unfortunately, that is not always an easy task.

I have always used stories to convey messages and this book will be no different. Some of the stories are about clients and some are my own personal experiences. A few of my client stories provide perfect illustrations that you can't always just take a professional's word for things. Who then can we trust?

A chapter 13 bankruptcy is where a debtor is permitted to keep most of their belongings, but they must make a monthly payment to a bankruptcy trustee for three to five years to pay as much as possible to their unsecured creditors. While in a chapter 13 plan, debtors are required to obtain permission from the bankruptcy court before entering into any new financial transactions such as purchasing a motor vehicle on credit, purchasing a home, or even refinancing a home.

Bankruptcy does not necessarily mean your financial life ceases to happen, but the bankruptcy court does monitor your transactions to make sure you are making wise decisions. It makes no sense to prohibit a person from replacing a motor vehicle if their vehicle becomes unreliable and the debtor can no longer rely upon the vehicle to get to work or get to other essential places like doctor appointments. If they can't get to work, they lose income, and the chapter 13 plan may fail. Without a car, they may even lose their job making it impossible to pay anything back to their creditors.

I once had a client who wanted to refinance her home. She was approached by a mortgage loan company about a loan. This is probably the first lesson to learn. People who approach you trying to sell you something are rarely the best option. Those in bankruptcy generally have a lower credit score so it is difficult to get a good interest rate. The loan officer who approached my client convinced her that she would be able to get a much better interest rate if only she would refinance with him now at a higher interest rate and make her payments for a year.

Part of our first lesson is everybody should **shop around,** don't fall for the first sales pitch. This client didn't talk to anybody else and did not question the advice. This is the second lesson: **question everything** you are told, always! You don't need to be belligerent with the people you work with but in the back of your mind you should always be asking yourself if what they are proposing makes sense and if this is available here, then is there a better deal somewhere else?

She was promised if she stayed current for a year on the new loan they would then refinance at a much better rate. When one of my bankruptcy debtors wanted to refinance, I had to prepare a motion to enter into a financial transaction and file it with the court. I needed the HUD documents to do that. The HUD documents disclose the interest rate, amount financed, term length, payment, where the funds will go, and the closing costs.

When I received her HUD documents and reviewed them it became apparent, she was being taken advantage of; her interest rate was higher than her current loan, her monthly payment was higher than her current loan and now she would have a longer term than her current loan. The question in the back of her mind should have been: *why do I need to stay current on a new loan rather than just staying current on the loan I already have?*

To be honest there are sometimes reasons that could be the case. Sometimes debtors refinance and use the loan proceeds to pay off their bankruptcy so they are no longer in a bankruptcy. That is often the case when a debtor is primarily using the bankruptcy plan to cure delinquent mortgage payments. That way they lower their monthly outlay making it easier to stay current on ongoing mortgage payments because they no longer have a bankruptcy payment. The mortgage payment may go up some, but they no longer have to make a bankruptcy payment resulting in a much lower monthly output. That was not the case with this client.

To be blunt, this client simply did not understand financial transactions. That is probably the hardest lesson for most people to accept. We can't know everything; seek expert advice.

I explained to her that the proposed loan was less desirable than what she already had and that there were many mortgage companies who would refinance for her after staying current on the mortgage payments she was already making without the need to refinance with a less favorable mortgage. She would have probably figured that out herself if she had just shopped around. Legitimate lenders would have told her if she just stayed current for a few more months she would likely qualify for their loan.

Her response was that her "guy", the loan officer, told her it was a good idea. She went back to her loan officer and relayed what I had explained to her. He had been caught but that did not deter him. He explained to her that while the payment was higher, the interest was higher, and it was a longer term, that is what she had to do in order to qualify for their lower interest rate loan in a year. That was just their "program" and the program was developed just to help people in her position.

She came back and relayed that information

to me and I said, great, get him to put that in writing and we would see if a bankruptcy judge would approve the transaction. She went back to the loan officer and he said he couldn't put it in writing because she may not qualify in a year because of non-compliance with the requirements. Her "guy" offered to come to my office to explain it to me.

I patiently listened all along knowing he was just a shyster. When he was done, I said it would be no problem as long as he put it in writing that she could get a lower interest rate in a year. He explained that he could not do that because she may not qualify in a year. When I said I understood but that he would at least have to put down in the contract that there was a program and if she complied with the terms of the program, she would be able to get the lower interest loan in a year. He got up and huffed away and my client went with him. That was a lesson I had learned long ago. Sometimes you lose clients doing what is best for them.

My client found another attorney who would

file the motion for her, and he substituted as her attorney. I happened to be in the courtroom on the day her motion came before the judge. Just as I had predicted the judge saw through the motion and it was denied. In the end, all she ended up doing was finding two shysters who wanted her money and, in the process, had to pay another bankruptcy attorney the fees required to prepare and attempt to prosecute the motion. Thankfully, the judge stopped her from having to pay the shyster loan officer.

That is a very important lesson: there are many shysters out there. Don't fall under their control. There is always a shyster who is willing and anxious to take your money.

Many of my clients had to file bankruptcies because they fell under the sway of a shyster. I had many clients who came to me because they could not make a car payment. They had bought a car with a very expensive payment because "the dealer told me I should be able to afford it." I heard that line so many times. Many of these were people who made $12.00 an hour and were talked into a

$600.00 a month (or more) car payment.

All it takes is simple math to understand that a person making a gross monthly wage of $2,080.00 per month most likely cannot afford a $600.00 monthly car payment. At least not if they are otherwise supporting a household. A person making $2,080.00 is generally paying about 15% in taxes. That eats up about $312.00 and housing is generally around $900.00 at a minimum. With a $600.00 car payment that leaves $268.00 per month for food, utilities, gas, vehicle maintenance, vehicle insurance, health insurance and a myriad of other expenses. Of course, wages have increased some, but prices are also even higher.

A car salesman kept a straight face when he told those buyers they could afford a car payment that high. They would have been much better off purchasing a more reasonable vehicle with a $300.00 car payment and even then they would have had a very tight budget.

The way to avoid shysters is to question

everything and do some research before even venturing out. Research is not the be all and end all of the process, but it is necessary. You may not understand everything but it will likely be enough for you to recognize signs that just don't sit right. Part of questioning everything is simply using common sense. It only takes a few minutes to go over a budget in your own mind. You don't have to take their word for anything. Remember, one of their goals is to earn a commission so they have incentive to sell you that car. Also, beware of the deal that is only available "right now.".

There are some things that should always sound alarms. Sometimes, there are reasons you have to enter into a contract right now but most of the time it is only because salespeople don't want to let you out of their sight until they have earned a commission. It doesn't hurt for you to understand their motive, and in most cases their motive is a commission.

Another almost sure sign of a shyster is when they make a promise of a future benefit that they **won't put in writing**. My client trying to refinance her home would have benefited if she had become a little suspicious when the salesman's promises were not in the proposed contract. Ask why the discussed terms aren't in the contract and understand if they aren't in the contract, it is because they are likely not going to happen.

It also does not hurt to question your own motives and sometimes reevaluate your motives. Where I practiced, we had a beloved sports franchise owned by a person who also owned numerous car dealerships. I was shocked at the number of bankruptcy clients who purchased a vehicle or wanted to purchase a vehicle from him because he had done so much for the community, and they "owed" it to him to support him.

Sometimes his deals were as good as everywhere else but often clients acknowledged they could have managed a better deal elsewhere. I had to explain to them that they were in bankruptcy or contemplating bankruptcy, and he was still a billionaire. When I put it in those terms, they began to understand they did not owe him anything and more importantly, they didn't have the luxury of being able to give him their unearned business. If you are going to shop somewhere, make them earn your business.

Chapter 1 Recap:

1. Be wary of sales people who approach you.
2. Shop around.
3. Question everything.
4. We can't know everything.
5. There are shysters out there.
6. Use common sense.
7. Watch for alarms.
8. Look at motives including your own.

Chapter 2

Prepare for a Healthy Financial Future

Wealthy people follow guidelines whether written or just in their head. While I am nowhere near being wealthy, I have been around wealthy people most of my life whether through work or through extended family who happened to have plenty of money. If I was going to name three things all of them seem to have in common, it would be:

1. Dedication
2. A little suspicion
3. A little bit ruthless

This book will not even attempt to discuss how to be somewhat ruthless. I am not even sure if that is something one develops or if that is just a trait with which one is born. I suspect both but I will let you figure that out. My purpose is to help you have a healthy financial future. That is not to say if you follow the lessons I am outlining that you won't become wealthy, because you just might. This section discusses how to have dedication and a healthy degree of suspicion. I am sure there are many traits one can develop beyond the scope of this book but if you will follow those herein you will be on the road to a financially stress-free life.

I have a relative who owns a small furniture store. He is not one of the super wealthy relatives, but his store provided him enough income to live a good life. My wife also has a great uncle who owns a small chain of banks. He isn't a billionaire but he is certainly does very well. He purchased a twin mattress from the furniture store and it had to be delivered. I happened to be at the furniture store and was asked if I would deliver the mattress. I happened to be with my brother at the time so the two of us delivered the mattress.

I'm not really sure if this falls under the category of being dedicated to having no waste or because he was just a little ruthless, but he got upset that my relative would waste money paying two delivery drivers when one could easily have delivered the small mattress. He did not know we were doing it for free. The point, however, is that it was his habit to cut out waste anywhere he could.

Step One-Build a Valuable Habit

A sound financial future is something that needs to be planned. Far too many of us let the situation guide us rather than making plans so we can guide the situation. When should we start our financial plans? Frankly, we should start our planning before we have money. For example, many churches encourage people to pay a tithe that is a percentage of their income. Children who are taught to pay their tithes from the moment they get their first allowance generally keep paying a tithing as adults. For every dollar they get, they contribute something to the church. This is a habit; it starts very early. Parents, teach your children the same lesson about **savings**.

Even if you didn't build healthy financial habits when you were young; it is never too late to start building effective habits. A comprehensive financial plan should start with a commitment to put a percentage of everything you earn in the bank for savings. There is no set or perfect percentage. The amount of money is not as important as the habit. Make a commitment and stick to it. The ultimate goal is to have enough liquid assets to weather the financial storms that happen to all of us. Once we have enough liquid assets, we can weather these storms and start to put the money into less liquid but more productive investments.

One dollar a week doesn't seem like much but it adds up. You aren't necessarily trying to get rich, although that could be the end result. Your initial goal, however, is to insulate yourself from financial crises. Most Americans are one small crisis away from a bankruptcy. Many of us could not come up with $300.00 to fix our car. Even that small crisis can have a domino effect. With no car it is difficult to get to work and missing work could lead to a loss of employment.

Many are only one car repair away from financial ruin but there are hundreds of other possible causes lurking in the background that may lead the house of cards to come crumbling down. It really doesn't take very much. A small $16.26 deposit each month earning an interest rate of 1% will be worth $1,000.00 in 5 years. A $100.00 deposit each month earning 1% will be worth $6,150.00. It might not be as easy to put away $100.00 per month. You might have to start with $5.00, $10.00 or even some other small amount.

Start somewhere and as you receive increases in pay, increase the amount you save. When I was first married it would have been difficult to put away $10.00 per month but now I can put away much more.

The first thought most of us have is: what money? Where do I find the money to put away? Most of us have some guilty pleasure in which we indulge. We all need a few guilty pleasures in life and somehow, we always find the money to indulge in those guilty pleasures. Mine was big gulps and travel. There was a time I drank five or more big gulps a day and somehow, I have been to almost every state in the United States multiple times and at least twenty-five foreign countries.

Those were my guilty pleasures: travel and big gulps. My wife occasionally points out how rich we would be if I had just cut out a few big gulps each day and one or two trips each year. I have probably averaged ten trips a year for the last fifty years. In my defense, I point out to her that I am not the one who loves Disneyland so much I am on first name basis with Mickey.

I cringe being an example of bad financial habits but if I had cut out two drinks a day for the last fifty years I could have saved about $36,000.00 and that is without interest. Add a few thousand for my travels expenses each year and that is a low estimate for two trips, and I could have $136,000.00 in the bank today and that doesn't include any interest. The worst part of that is I no longer buy two-dollar big gulps, I now buy $5.00 chai tea lattes.

Granted, I could have used some of that

money to resolve the financial problems that have popped up that I had to put on credit cards and pay an exorbitant amount of interest. Having those funds available would have saved me a lot of interest that would have far exceeded the amount of the crisis and I could have put away even more money. My $136,000.00 would likely be more like $200,000 to $300,000 by now. Oh well, that is water under the bridge.

You will be surprised at how much money you do spend on guilty pleasures. You don't have to cut them all out, but do cut back a little. Using me as an example again, I could have had three big gulps instead of five and I could have averaged eight trips rather than ten trips. I would have still enjoyed big gulps and I would have still enjoyed a lot of travel. This is not about giving up every guilty pleasure in your life; but saving a little for pater.

Do you buy a big gulp every day? A Starbucks coffee? Giving up one big gulp or one cup of coffee a week is a start. Do you drink alcohol? A 6-pack a week could just as easily be a

5-pack a week. I realize a 5-pack is not available at the local mini mart. Follow the lead of the cell phone companies that allows their customers to carry-over minutes from one month to the next month. Buy a 6-pack and have one carry over to the next week. Every 6 weeks you will save the cost of a 6-pack. At the price of beer, saving the amount of one six-pack is no small amount. If you drink a 12-pack a week; carry-over 2 into the next week. You don't need me to tell you where to save. Just realize there is somewhere you can carve out a few dollars a week to put away. Make the decision to do it!

Now, putting something away is just half the equation. Use your talents to bring in a little more income. My father-in-law was a fantastic piano player. He spent almost every Saturday night playing in a band at a local restaurant. He didn't make much each night but in a month, it was somewhere between $300 and $500. He did that for about sixty years. Even if it was only $300 per month that amounts to $216,000 without interest.

Not all of us have that kind of talent. But we

all have different talents. I have heard of people who knitted caps and sold one a month. Many moons ago I had a neighbor who would build small flat trailers. He would build a small 5'x 7' single axle trailer every 6 months or so. Current laws and a litigious society have made that a little harder to do but there are still little projects that can bring in extra money. My father-in-law made an extra few thousand dollars a year and that was in the early 1970s. If he put that money in a bank he would have at least $100,000 today and that is without taking into account interest and inflation.

I know another guy who just decided he was going to learn how to make jewelry. He makes a piece or two each week. It didn't take a lot of time, but he sells each piece for about $35.00. After expenses that is about $125.00 per month he could put away. I don't know if he does but it is a great way to save.

My daughter started what she called Beckee's Deals. She shared deals in Omaha, Nebraska where her husband was in medical school.

They had no money and struggled. As she got more followers, manufacturers would send her toys and other products for her to review, and she got to keep the toys and products. That provided Christmas and birthday presents and parties for their children through his 9 years of medical school and residency. That saved them a lot of money. On top of that, she also saved a lot of money because she took the time to know the deals for things she had to purchase.

We all know people who work overtime. We all need to have our living expenses in line with our regular income. That means overtime is for things we want, and not for needs, and we all have wants. I always told my clients to base their budget on just their regular pay and treat the overtime as a bonus. Spend half the bonus on things they desire and the other half goes in the bank.

The point is find that something you can do to make a little extra money. It may even have to be something that takes very little time and only makes a little money but even a little money adds up.

I have a brother who started a business many decades ago. We are all afraid of the other shoe dropping. He was no different, so he never spent money. He found an accountant he explicitly trusted and let him deal with the money. He went merrily on his way running a business and only took a modest draw. He did that for many years allowing the money to accumulate just in case the other shoe dropped. It wasn't like he was living poorly but he was also not living the rich life.

He was meeting with his accountant and told him he wanted to increase the amount of money he took in a draw and wondered if that was wise. His accountant shocked him. He told him he could take whatever he wanted. As he grew his business he acquired equipment, supplies, contracts, and more importantly, he had put away enough money he was now immune from the shoe dropping. He was actually pretty well off; some would say he is rich. If he wanted, he could sell his business for a lot of money. Of course, he didn't want to sell. As he told me, the business is making too much money to want to sell.

Most of my clients could be described as gluttons. They never learned to control their urges. Don't give up on your desires but do control them; don't let them control you.

Recap:

1. Put something away each pay—build a valuable habit.
2. Find a way to earn a little more.

Step Two: Understand expenses and budget

Budgets are always a good idea. There are a few times in an academic pursuit where something is indelibly planted in our minds. I will never forget one professor's words. He said that there is one simple basic truth. In all economies, there are a finite amount of resources. A country's economy is simply the laws, rules, and policies that encourage the best use of the finite resources that are available. Just like a country, we have a finite number of resources. Our resources are usually the wages that we earn. A personal budget is simply our own set of rules and policies that we implement to get the best possible use of our finite resources.

People filing bankruptcy are required to file a budget on Official Form 106I and 106J. In a bankruptcy filing, I had to help clients understand how to budget well enough that they can successfully complete a bankruptcy plan. We should all be able to budget enough to deal with every day financial issues. The earlier example of clients purchasing far too expensive vehicles touched on budgets but only superficially. Businesses and individuals starting a business understand how to set up a realistic budget. At least the ones that are successful know how to budget. Every good business plan includes a budget.

The truth is budgets are very individual; a budget that is realistic for one person isn't necessarily reasonable for another person. Even when it seems like all things are equal, a budget item that is reasonable for one person isn't always the right approach for another person.

When putting a budget together for a bankruptcy filing, it is imperative that the trustee and the judge believe it is a realistic budget for that person. Consequently, budget discretion is often limited because clients are seeking protection from their creditors through the bankruptcy process and are required to comply with other people's beliefs of what constitutes a reasonable expense. For example, a chapter 13 trustee could balk at an expensive vehicle in the bankruptcy plan that the trustee considers a luxury rather than a necessity.

The general population is not so restricted. You may want an expensive vehicle and the main criteria as to whether you can obtain one is whether it will fit in your budget. Nobody is going to question your budget for reasonableness and your desire for a nice vehicle may be reasonable. A vehicle may or may not be considered a luxury in a bankruptcy plan depending upon the purpose for which the vehicle is used. A good example is a construction worker who needs a 3/4 ton truck because he is required to haul heavy equipment back and forth between the shop and the job site. In order to make money that is necessary to meet the obligations of the plan, he must have this vehicle.

Rather than waiting until you are facing a dire financial situation, **now** is the time to look at your budget. Look now while you still have wide discretion as to what you believe are your own preferences. As I stated earlier, I love traveling and have been willing to forgo a few other things in order to be able to travel. I don't live in an excessively expensive home and I don't drive an expensive vehicle. I do however, live in a decent home and drive a respectable vehicle. As a matter of fact, I drive a Hyundai because that is a reasonably priced vehicle that is also dependable.

There are no Porsches in my past and it is unlikely any will be in my future. Hopefully, however, I will be able to visit Greece again someday. Greece may not be in your immediate future but it is not an impossibility down the road if that is what you want to do. Each of our desires is different. The point is that you need to determine what is important to you and then put together a budget that allows the things that are important to you to be within your reach. To do that, you need to get control of the money you have unless you make so much money you couldn't spend all of your income. Even then, you should still budget.

The thing to understand about budgets is that they are not easy to put together and are not even self-explanatory. Implementing a budget is not always easy either. A budget almost always requires us to put off instant gratification for an even greater amount of gratification later in life. That reminds me of a scene in a popular television series. There are a couple of nerdy geniuses who are roommates in an apartment across the hall from a beautiful girl that one of the geniuses really likes. In one scene, she is having a party and her old boyfriend shows up and causes problems and the nerdy genius leaves the party and goes across the hall to his apartment.

The girl comes over to apologize and ends up crying on his shoulder and that leads from one thing to another and soon they are kissing. At that point he asks her how much she had to drink and points out that it may be the alcohol leading to the kiss more than long lasting attraction. She thinks about it a minute and tells him he is so smart, and his reply is a sarcastic yeah, "I'm a friggin genius." In other words, he understood a one-night stand may mean he is giving up a more solid future with her and that is his real goal. As you cut back on a few guilty pleasures, understand that you are doing so in order to have a more solid financial future.

Most financial advisors advise people to sit down and write a budget and then experiment to *see* if it is realistic as you try to implement it. Once you determine how realistic or unrealistic it is, they advise you to adjust it. While putting together a budget is a critically important step towards financial independence, don't do it without a little perspective. Take your checkbook or debit card transaction records and enter them into a spreadsheet so you can see where you are currently spending your money. If you are on a cash basis, start by keeping all your receipts and record them into a spreadsheet.

While you are acquiring receipts, notice what you are doing with your money and try cutting back on unnecessary and wasteful spending. If you pull into 7-11 to purchase gas and get the urge to buy a Big Gulp, ask yourself if the purpose of the Big Gulp is one of those necessary guilty pleasures or is it just something you are buying out of habit. All of us have purchasing habits that do not actually satisfy a need as much as they satisfy an impulse.

Some of our purchasing habits are worthwhile and essential, but many are unnecessary and excessive. As I previously stated I was drinking about five Big Gulps a day. It never even occurred to me that I didn't need that many Big Gulps. As a matter of fact, when I started paying attention, I realized I was constantly throwing away half-full cups just to go in and get a "fresh" Big Gulp. I was stunned at how little thought I put into my Big Gulp habit. I was following my regular routine; throw away one cup (with soda still in the cup) just to go in and get a new one. It never occurred to me that I could simply refill the cup I already had. After all, a refill costs` about half as much as a new cup. I had been wasting money for years.

Preparing a budget would have done two things. First, I would have realized how much money I was spending on Big Gulps. I was spending over $300.00 per month just on Big Gulps. Upon that realization I might have started to look for better ways to satisfy my guilty pleasure and I may have realized I could have cut that expense in half simply by reusing my cup.

You and I probably have something in common. I didn't recognize my bad Big Gulp spending habit until somebody else recognized it and pointed it out to me. The reason I did not think about it was because I did not have a budget. You probably don't recognize your own less than optimal spending habits. It may not even be a bad spending habit. It may just be a spending habit that isn't optimal. My Big Gulp habit is an example of the two ways that we need to look at our spending habits. Looking backwards does a few things for us. First, it lets us know where we spend our money and second, we will find that there are some spending entries that will even shock our own conscience. I said I love traveling. Looking at my travel expenses in the past shocked me. If I had saved half the money I spent on traveling I would have been able to save a lot of money. I may even be rich. In other words, I was shocked at what I was spending.

Travel was no different. It wasn't until I saw

how much I was really spending that I took steps to reduce my traveling expense. In the end, traveling a little less often and a little less extravagantly improved my life. I realized that I was traveling so much that the enjoyment was reduced. If you eat steak all the time, pretty soon steak isn't a treat anymore. I was once in London and was so bored being there again that I actually paid to change my ticket so I could go home a day earlier.

Travel can get so commonplace that eventually every big city is the same. I had a five-year period where I traveled about 150 times a year. At that time much of it was for a business project. It got to the point I had to look at a phone to see what area code I was in so I would remember where I was. I am certain that would never have occurred if I had to stay within a budget.

When I was a teenager, I had a friend who had more money than he knew what to do with. Somehow, we usually figured out ways to spend it. For about a six-month period we decided we were going to eat steak for breakfast and dinner and even sometimes at lunchtime. While it was an enjoyable guilty pleasure for a while it just became routine. While most people salivate over a good steak, to this day I just think of it as an uneventful piece of meat. Our guilty indulgence habits can become so much they are just habits and often no longer enjoyable. I no longer drink Big Gulps and rarely eat steaks. You may find you have guilty pleasures have likewise just turned into habits so you should be able to break the habit and save money.

The next important concept to understand is that we are sometimes not the best person to determine what is a valid "guilty pleasure." Keep an open mind. I didn't enlist anybody's help so they would point out to me how much I was wasting simply by not refilling my Big Gulp cup. Maybe I should have solicited help. They were able to see something I wasn't able to see. This is especially important if we have spending habits that might border on the irrational just as my teenage steaks bordered on the irrational.

The Diagnostic and Statistical Manual of

Mental Disorders identifies a number of habits that are worthy of concern; many are those where we don't want to or can't admit there is a problem. The most obvious of these types of habits are gambling, compulsive shopping, and while it may not actually be identified in the Diagnostic and Statistical Manual of Mental Disorders, gullibility. Nobody wants to admit they are addicted to gambling or are a compulsive shopper and people really don't want to admit to being gullible.

Nevertheless, a good part of what I did as a bankruptcy attorney was to point out these types of behaviors to clients. I even had to tell a few prospective clients I would not file a case for them if they were still facing the very same issues that led them into my office. The first step towards financial freedom is realizing there is a bad habit and then taking steps to overcome the bad habit. A good attorney wants to help clients overcome bad habits. An attorney working with financial matters has not helped the client if they recognized a bad financial habit and did not point it out to them. Often clients who are not adequately advised just return to bad habits leading them again into uncontrollable debt. Budgets are a good way to recognize bad habits and gullible behavior.

I had a couple come into my office to file a bankruptcy because they had "invested" money with a foreign company and the investment fell through. We discussed the investment and they assured me that they had learned their lesson: they had not. We filed a chapter 13 bankruptcy, and they came into my office because they could not make their payments. The court will sometimes abate payment which essentially means you don't have to make the missed payments.

The court is pretty understanding the first, and even the second time a debtor wants to abate a payment. The third time the Court wants to know more specifically about what happened that made them unable to make the payment. The two previous times they stated it was because they had work problems and lost some income. This time I asked them to bring me copies of their pay stubs to show the court. They brought me the pay stubs hoping nobody would really notice but they had not actually missed any pay, so I asked them what was really happening.

That is when they admitted they had put more money in the foreign investment because they were told that was the only way to make the company successful so their investment would be able to make money. They were convinced they would not even need the bankruptcy once their investment income began rolling in.

As we discussed the investment it became obvious, they were investing with con men from Nigeria. It was well known there were Nigerian con artists conning Americans out of their money. I was surprised they were so gullible, but I could not convince them it was a con game. I eventually called the attorney general's fraud department and explained the "investment" to them and asked if they would speak to my clients. The attorney general's office told them point blank they were con artists. They assured me they would never invest in the con again and we prepared a motion to abate and explained it to the court and assured the court they would not be so gullible in the future. The motion was granted, and the missed payments were abated.

A few months later they missed more payments but did not call me when they received the motion to dismiss their case and would not respond to my calls. Their case was dismissed for non-payment. Many months later they came back into my office to see if they could refile and explained they were done with the Nigerians. Being somewhat suspicious I asked them for the last six months bank statements.

When I got the bank statement there were a few unexplained deposits and withdrawals of thousands of dollars. Of course, that sounded the alarms. Where did they get that kind of money and where did it go? When it was all flushed out they had been taking funds out of their 401k retirement account and continued to invest with the Nigerians. In about a years' time they invested about $100,000 from their 401k retirement account in the Nigerian scheme.

Just as gambling is an addiction that needs to be treated, so is this kind of gullibility. I told them I would not file their case until they obtained treatment to ensure they knew not to be so gullible again. They later told me they thought the figure was much closer to $25,000 and did not realize how much money they had lost. The important message is that if they had prepared a budget from their bank statements, they would have realized how much money they had been spending. Sometimes we just go on auto pilot with our finances, and we don't even know how much or where our money goes. So what do you do if you are not filing a bankruptcy and you don't have anybody who is specifically tasked with looking at your finances and providing you guidance?

Hopefully, you won't ever be in that position. That does not mean, however, that you wouldn't benefit from someone else's input. Regardless of whether you are married or single, you should find a trusted confidante who will look over your shoulder and give you some guidance. Often a couple's bad spending habits are acceptable or at least not noticed by both spouses and another person's input would be helpful. This person is someone you must trust completely, perhaps a religious leader, parent, sibling, adult child, or possibly even a best friend. While some of us may rely on best friends, we need to be careful. Frankly, no matter who we choose we need to be careful. It should go without saying but discussions about your finances do not need and should not include sharing private information such as social security numbers. If you want a friend's advice about a contract and want them to read it make a copy and black out private information. This may be marriage advice more than financial advice but if you are a couple, make sure this person isn't going to be viewed as favoring one spouse over another.

This is an area where I am likely to give you advice that is different from the advice you would get from a typical financial planner. A financial planner is likely to tell you to share everything with him or her and then he will tell you where you could improve based upon what was learned in the few minutes or hour that you spent there. And of course, a financial planner's advice comes with a price tag and his own agenda. Often his agenda will be to set up a program he has to monitor and of course, monitoring that will cost you money. Sometimes that makes sense but if at all possible, right now is not a good time to increase your expenses.

A trusted confidante can often times give you more insight because they are able to observe you more often. They don't just look at your spending for an hour or two and then dish out their advice. The best advice isn't really advice at all. It is when somebody points out something to you and *YOU* make the decision as to how you wish to deal with the issue. You are much more likely to follow a course of action you have decided to undertake rather than something somebody else is *forcing* on you. The will, however, only work if you keep an open mind and think about what has been suggested.

We need to realize that budgeting requires communication. That is especially so for couples. When I turned nineteen, I got a job working for the federal government. During the almost 4 years I worked for the government I accumulated a retirement fund. When I quit the retirement fund was paid to me. If course, I had to take a penalty in taxes to get the funds but after doing so I received a check for $3,500.00. That was in 1979 and it was a lot of money. I had been married for a just under two years and we thought we were rich.

I decided to use the money to pay off a few bills and the rest for a vacation to visit Ohio, the state where I was born. I moved to Utah when I was eight years old. I spent from eight to twenty-three telling people I wasn't a Utahn, I was a Buckeye so I wanted to return to my roots if just for a vacation. Utah and Ohio, or at least the part of Ohio where I was born are very different from each other. Utah is a well educated conservative state while the area I was from in Ohio was much less educated and largely a blue-collar steel mill town. I learned a lot on that trip. The first was that even though I had been a Buckeye my whole life, I came back to Utah realizing I wasn't a Buckeye, I was a Utahn. While I loved my heritage the saying that you can't go home again rang true to me. I was no longer a Buckeye.

The second lesson I learned on that trip was that a husband and wife should communicate with each other. I had spent my $3,500 retirement on a vacation and paid off some of our bills while my wife had bought a few other things and paid off a few other bills. We had done two different things with the money, and we were in trouble. We had to call parents and borrow $2,500, the amount that we spent differently. Luckily, a few of the bills we both paid just refunded the overpayment back to us.

Recap:

1. Understand your expenses and create a budget; be dedicated.
2. Seek help recognizing financial downfalls; a little suspicion goes a long ways.
3. Communicate!

Step Three: Remedies short of bankruptcy

Occasionally, our finances are in such distress that our options are limited, and we start to look for a solution that requires professional help. The obvious solutions are credit counseling, debt settlement and maybe even bankruptcy. Let me give my caveat before we get too far into this discussion. I practiced in the area of bankruptcy law for many years. Often, by the time I get to see people, the credit counseling and debt settlement attempts have already failed. Consequently, over the years I have developed a bias against companies that only provide credit counseling and debt settlement.

Conversely, I have practiced in the area of bankruptcy long enough to know that bankruptcy is not always the best option either. I realized that to help people, I couldn't limit my practice to just bankruptcy or just debt settlement or any one area. I didn't want my own interests to limit the options available to my clients. I looked at an individual's financial situation and then made recommendations that were the most helpful to my clients. That may be debt settlement, cleaning up a credit report, and yes, even bankruptcy when it is the best option. It is important that an attorney look at the overall financial picture so he or she can make recommendations that will help the client survive their financial distress. All options must be on the table.

That is the lesson for you also. Keep options on the table. Many of my clients came into my office and "inform" me of what they need. With very limited knowledge they make a decision, and they want to stick with it. One client came into my office and told me he wanted a chapter 7 bankruptcy and nothing else. I did a nationwide search of bankruptcy courts as I always did and found that his social security number was associated with a bankruptcy in California. I always had prospective clients fill out a one-page questionnaire and one of the questions is have you filed a bankruptcy in the last 8 years? He had written that he had not.

The bankruptcy law does not permit more than one chapter 7 within a certain period of time. When I informed him of that he said I was wrong because he read on the internet that the courts never look in other jurisdictions. The bankruptcy was old enough that all he really had to do was wait a few months to be eligible, but he was facing a civil trial that required some kind of immediate action. There were solutions but he would have nothing of them. I could have simply filed a motion to continue the trial date. The courts are generally willing to allow at least one continuance. That way his bankruptcy would have aged enough he would be eligible to file thus avoiding the trial. It was just a few months.

The bankruptcy courts do check national records and I told him that. He wanted me to look at the web page where he got the information, so I did. The page was written by an untrained "paralegal" who learned all he had to know by reading the bankruptcy code. Reading the bankruptcy code makes as much sense as reading Isaiah in the Bible the first time. Without some background Isaiah makes no sense and neither does the bankruptcy code. It takes a fundamental understanding of the law as well as case law to make any sense of the bankruptcy code. In fact, attorneys who do not practice in the area of bankruptcy don't generally want to even try handling a bankruptcy.

The code isn't what gave him the idea because the code is so clear and direct to anybody knowledgeable about the bankruptcy code. 11 U.S. Code § 727(8) says:

> ***(a)****The court shall grant the debtor a discharge, unless—*
>
> *(8)the debtor has been granted a discharge under this section, under section 1141 of this title, or under section 14, 371, or 476 of the Bankruptcy Act, in a case commenced within 8 years before the date of the filing of the petition;*

The code says nothing about jurisdictions so it does take a little knowledge and some case law to understand. I was willing to provide him with cases that interpreted the law but he was convinced and did not want to hear anything else. The paralegal was just a shyster who was trying to get away with something. His goal was to convince the people who read his web page that the bankruptcy code was so simple they could file their own bankruptcy. Nothing could be further from the truth. It is not wise to file a bankruptcy without an attorney. There are far too many potential minefields in the bankruptcy code. The paralegal could not do it for them because he was not an attorney, but he was offering to sell them the forms needed to file on their own. Never mind that the forms are on every court's webpage for free. He was selling them for $129.00. As we discussed earlier, there are shysters out there and we should all have at least a small degree of suspicion. This cried out for a lot of suspicion.

It is conceivable a court could fail to find a debtor's chapter 7 bankruptcy in another jurisdiction. Afterall, bankruptcy courts are staffed by mere humans who are not perfect. But even if the court did not pick up on the previous filing, the trustee or one of the creditors almost certainly would have. All three generally check.

Unfortunately, paralegals and sometimes not all attorneys have enough bankruptcy knowledge to know they have to check in all jurisdictions. Many also do not have the technology required to check national bankruptcy records. There are even attorneys who simply are willing to risk it because that technology costs money. Afterall, they generally get paid upfront. Whatever the reason, some attorneys don't catch the previous bankruptcy and will file the case. The potential client found one such attorney even though I told him it was against the bankruptcy code, and he was extremely unlikely to get away with it. I even told him it would cost him a great deal more if he came back to me to try to fix the problem.

Nevertheless, he came back to me when he received the trustee's motion to dismiss with prejudice. The other attorney told him they were right, and his only option was to allow the case to be dismissed with prejudice. That wasn't actually correct but his only cure at that point was to convert to a chapter 13 bankruptcy where he would be required to make a payment for a three to five year period and of course, the attorney fees to deal with the motion to dismiss with prejudice and a chapter 13 far exceeded what they would have been if he had just come into my office with an open mind.

I would not have been offended if he said he wanted to get another opinion and asked another bankruptcy attorney if that was true. Even the attorney who did file the case would have told him he could not file if he had let him know about the previous bankruptcy.

Another potential client come into my office seeking a chapter 7 bankruptcy. Again, they only wanted a chapter 7 and were reluctant to discuss any other options. Just as in the previous case I had them fill out a one-page bankruptcy questionnaire. In the questionnaire I ask if they own a home, car or any other secured property and if so, how much they were worth and how much was owed on each. I asked how much they owed in unsecured debt and tax debt. The form also asked about income and assets. While the form sounds ominous it is not. It usually takes clients only a few minutes to fill it out but it gives me a good picture of their financial position.

This potential client owned a home with a small amount of equity and owned a vehicle that was worth about $6,000 and he listed $25,000 in unsecured debt. He also had $3,500 in the bank. Other than the $25,000 in debt he was in pretty good shape.

After discussing his debt it became obvious he had been working hard to dig himself out of debt but could not deal with two creditors. I found he had spent the last two years paying off his creditors but could not make headway with the two creditors. In talking further, I noticed that the two creditors were payday lender type of businesses that were charging more than 45% interest and further the "unsecured debt", unbeknownst to him was actually secured debt on his vehicle.

We will discuss the specifics about

bankruptcy in a later chapter but suffice it to say he would have lost his vehicle and the $3,500 in a chapter 7 bankruptcy, and he desperately needed his vehicle. His options for keeping his vehicle were to either file a chapter 13 bankruptcy or negotiate the debt. The $3,500 in the bank would be gone regardless of which option he chose.

We will further discuss this in a later chapter, but the lesson is to keep your mind open and be willing to listen to what options may be available to you. It wasn't just people wanting chapter 7 bankruptcies.

I had another potential client who wanted to file a chapter 13 because she was told by friends that people lose their homes in a chapter 7 bankruptcy. She did have a home but there was not a lot of equity in the home and she was current on payments. Debtors can often keep homes in a chapter 7 bankruptcy. The debtors who lose their homes are the ones who have more equity than they are allowed to keep. The bankruptcy code allows each state to create their own exemptions. Debtors are allowed to keep equity up to the amount of their state's exemption.

We all remember O. J. Simpson. He had a home in California but moved to Florida when he was sued. The reason is because Florida had an unlimited exemption for equity in a home while California had a limited exemption and he was being sued. There are essentially two reasons to file a chapter 13 in order to save a home. The first is if the equity exceeds the exemption and the second is to cure a mortgage delinquency through the chapter 13 plan. This client had neither reason for filing a chapter 13.

Luckily, this client had a healthy degree of suspicion. While she was set on filing a chapter 13, she also was not going to decide on an attorney without talking to more than one attorney. There is a major cost difference in filing a chapter 7 versus a chapter 13. I was the second attorney she spoke with. The first one was an attorney who almost always talked clients into chapter 13 cases because he made more money from a chapter 13 case. I just happened to give different advice and explained why the house would not be lost even in a chapter 7 bankruptcy. I didn't make as much money from the client as I would have by pushing them into a chapter 13 plan but I did do what was in the client's best interest.

The lesson is don't go to a law firm that only handles bankruptcy or debt settlement. There are firms that only do bankruptcy. There are even firms who only handle chapter 7 bankruptcies and firms that only handle chapter 13 bankruptcy. Additionally, there are even firms who only handle debt settlement. Surprise, surprise, somehow the clients that come into their office always need just the type of case they handle. Of course that is not always true but that is what they generally received.

While I have been discussing bankruptcy specifically, this lesson applies to all of us even if bankruptcy is not being considered. The best example I have is a client who came into my office wanting me to wind down his business. He was not personally liable on any of the debt and there was not any substantial equipment he would lose but he still thought creditors could come after him so in the wind-down period he wanted me to negotiate settlements with the creditors and he intended to contribute whatever funds were required for the settlements.

There are times when creditors can go after the owner of business entities but those times are pretty limited. After discussing all of the issues I explained to him that he was not personally liable on any of the debt and suggested the company simply file a chapter 7 bankruptcy. The company owed over a hundred thousand dollars to creditors and even settling for pennies on the dollar he would have still had to pay thousands of dollars. Companies do not receive a discharge but there is nothing to go after once the estate is administered. Essentially, a company dies with a chapter 7 bankruptcy. By filing a bankruptcy he did not have to put any money into the company to settle remaining debt and the bankruptcy did not personally affect his credit. His only cost was for my services and that was far less than any settlement we could have reached.

There were times I gave a client an idea they never thought was possible and this was one of those times. I have had clients who had a lot of equity in their homes but couldn't handle the monthly payments on the debts they had and thought their only hope was a chapter 13 bankruptcy. They had made the decision they would not qualify for a loan on their home. A home loan would have had much lower costs than a chapter 13 bankruptcy. In a chapter 13 bankruptcy they are paying attorney fees as well as up to 10% of each payment to the trustee to administer the bankruptcy plan. Remember, keep an open mind. They simply did not research a home loan because they thought it would be impossible. I told them to get a list of mortgage companies and call every one of them until they could obtain a loan. If they were unsuccessful then they should come back to me to file a bankruptcy.

They did come back to my office but not to

file a bankruptcy. They wanted to thank me for giving them worthwhile advice that ended up saving them a lot of money. Me being the pushy person I am, I took the opportunity to convince them to make greater payments than were required so they could get it paid off faster and then start putting some of that money away each month since they were used to living without it. They could put half away and spend the other half to improve their lives.

Sometimes the solution is not obvious or even easy. I had a client who could not get a home loan so I talked one of the creditors into giving him a loan for enough money that he could do debt settlement with the rest of the creditors. The lender was able to convert his loan into a secured loan by lending some additional funds needed to settle the remaining debt for pennies on the dollar. It is amazing, when a creditor hears bankruptcy sometimes pennies on the dollar is a good deal for them.

I have probably spent far too much time on

this issue but the point is to keep your options open. Don't foreclose possibilities because you prematurely make up your mind. Also, find a firm who will look at your overall finances and can represent you with whatever solution is best for you. That should be the case long before you consider bankruptcy. Most of my clients could have resolved their issues long before bankruptcy was needed if only they had sought legal advice before the situation was dire. The time to seek advice is when you first notice signs of financial trouble.

There are many firms that handle all types of financial issues including business formation, contracts, property sales, debt negotiation, credit repair, and even bankruptcy. All are interrelated and easily handled by one firm. The last thing you want to do is go to a firm that only handles one kind of case thus foreclosing all other options. Even when bankruptcy is the best option the firm should be able to also handle credit repair and restoration for you to repair your credit when the bankruptcy is complete. In previous case where the debtor had

$3,500 in the bank we chose debt negotiation. We simply called their creditors and told them their option was to either settle for a few cents on the dollar or we would have no choice but to file bankruptcy. We were able to settle the debts without even using all of the cash in the bank. The creditors choose wisely and our client was able to avoid a bankruptcy.

This is a good time to give my caveat: I rarely handled debt settlement and there is a major difference between debt negotiation and debt settlement. Both resolve debts without a bankruptcy but debt settlement simply sets up payment plans with creditors and then monitors those plans for a fee. You make a monthly payment to the firm who then makes payment to your creditors. Again, we will discuss bankruptcy in a later chapter, but I always believed debt settlement was simply a chapter 13 bankruptcy without the force of law. I also believed they rarely succeeded. I had several clients who made payments in a debt settlement plan for years only to file bankruptcy when the plan failed.

The most pressing reason for not liking debt settlement plans is because they do nothing you can't do on your own. Debt settlement firms simply write letters or call your creditors to see if they are willing to set up a payment plan to pay some or all of the debt. In the end, a few of your creditors agree to payment of a reduced amount over time, a few agree to one hundred percent of the debt paid over time without interest and some of them simply set up a payment of one-hundred percent of the debt with some interest. You could do that on your own and save a lot of fees. I have had many clients where I suggested they at least attempt that on their own at no cost to them before we choose to do anything else. Some successfully resolved their debt and came back in and thanked me for the idea while a few were unable to obtain agreement from their creditors and then we pursued other ideas. The more creditors one has the less likely a settlement can be reached with enough of them to make a viable plan but it is worth a try. They were in no worse condition, and we simply choose one of the other options.

Debt negotiation is often the best option. Debt settlement and debt negotiation are really distinctions I made within my own office because both are settlements, and both are negotiations. In my office I labeled negotiations where we used a lump sum to settle debts as a "debt negotiation." The complaint I have with debt settlement firms is that, overall, they specialize in debt settlement and only debt settlement. They only earn money if they convince the client to attempt debt settlement. They take a commission from each payment you make and their commission comes out first.

Often, people come to me after the debt settlement attempts have failed and as I look at individual cases, I can't understand how anybody thought a debt settlement plan would have worked. On the other hand, I had clients who came to my office seeking help with credit restoration after they finished their bankruptcy and I wonder why they didn't just do a debt negotiation. They had either the funds or assets to have had a successful debt negotiation and the crisis would have been over and they could have moved on.

The reason to choose a firm who handles everything is because you want to do what your circumstances warrant, not just what that firm offers. That is the reason a large percentage of debt settlement attempts fail. The only apparent reason they attempted a debt settlement is because the debt settlement company only makes money from the client if they signed on the dotted line to a debt settlement plan. Admitting the potential client would be better off with another option means they have to send the client away and they don't make any money. I am not, per se, opposed to debt settlement but not everybody that inquires about debt settlement can actually benefit from such services. Many, if not most, struggle through debt settlement for as long as they can (usually just long enough for the company to have made as much money as they could from the client) and finally end up filing a bankruptcy anyway.

If you are considering debt settlement, I recommend you retain an attorney who is willing to look at a wide range of options and, if appropriate, use the threat of a bankruptcy if the creditor isn't willing to negotiate a settlement. The threat of a bankruptcy is usually a hollow threat if it comes from a firm that exclusively does debt settlement. Understand, you need to be prepared to actually file for bankruptcy if settlement negotiations don't work.

The key to any negotiation is that you have to be able to bring something of value to the table. In debt settlement, that something of value usually is the promise to pay over time and a showing that you have the ability to make an ongoing payment. In debt negotiation it is usually a lump sum to pay to the creditor. That is why debt negotiation was a good solution for the client that only had a few debts and $3,500 in the bank.

Debt settlement is often accepted by creditors even though they know the plan will often fail. The mere fact a creditor accepts the plan is not necessarily an indication the plan will work. They accept the plan because they receive payments they would not have otherwise received had you simply filed a bankruptcy. Sometimes, however, if the creditor feels like they are just delaying the inevitable and the payments are not enough to warrant their interest they are unlikely to want to negotiate a settlement.

You need to be realistic with what you are attempting to accomplish. That brings up an important factor. You need to work with a debt settlement company that also has a realistic idea of what they think they can accomplish. If you want to seek the services of a debt settlement company, go to them prepared and with a little knowledge behind you. I have heard of debt settlement companies that tell clients they can settle $100,000.00 worth of debt with payments as little as $100.00 a month. There is an old adage that applies here:

If it sounds too good to be true;
It probably is!

You also need to be upfront and honest with

an attorney. I have had clients who outline all of their debts only to come up with more debts along the way. That makes it a lot harder to put together and maintain a viable plan.

The next thing you need to be careful about is that whatever is negotiated ***it must be in writing***. I was always shocked at the number of clients who made payments into a plan only to get close to the end to find out the creditor "changed their mind" and now wanted more payments or a lump sum payment. That is generally when they filed their bankruptcy. One would think an attorney would know a written contract was a good thing. They put a ton of paperwork in front of you to sign and most clients just sign them.

Bankruptcy is no different. We had a lot of documents for the clients. We always went over each document with the clients. That should be a warning sign to every potential client. If you are handed a stack of papers and just told to read them and sign them knowing the few seconds they gave you to sign them was not enough time to read and understand them then don't sign them. Ask that they go over each document with you so you know what is in them and you should read through them as they go over them. No matter what kind of solution you choose, make sure you understand everything. That is an important point, **read and understand everything**. One of my frustrations as an attorney was when I was going over documents and the client's mind was far away and without even an ounce of consideration at what they just signed.

A debt settlement company that appears to be saying anything they think you want to hear is probably more interested in getting your money than they are in settling your debts. Most reputable debt settlement companies work on a modified commission basis. You pay some amount down and further fees are based upon their performance. Far too often, debt settlement companies take a commission right off the top of what you are paying them. For every $100.00 you pay, they get to skim off anywhere between 10 to 50% before they even make a payment to a creditor. It should go without saying, if they are skimming off 50% you should go elsewhere.

They may have worked out "deals" with a few of your creditors and are paying a bulk of the payments to those few creditors. Many of the debt settlement firms have creditors they have a working relationship with so they treat them very well. Any agreement you have with a debt settlement firm should outline exactly how the funds are going to be used and how each creditor is going to be paid. I have seen some of those agreements that are so confusing I had a hard time following them. They had inconsistencies and broad unenforceable terms that always seemed to work to their advantage.

I once saw an agreement that actually had "the client acknowledges and understands that the creditor can terminate the agreement at any time and demand immediate payment in full." I would hope anybody reading that agreement would realize they should walk away. This client, however, was completely surprised by that statement in the contract. He had never read the contract and that was not what they had told him. **Read contracts and agreements** before signing.

You may be thinking that this example does not apply to you because you aren't in bankruptcy or even financial distress. Neither were many of my clients until they were taken advantage of by somebody who relied on the fact they would not read the contract. Many of my bankruptcy clients purchased some item or property where the salesperson told them they could pay off the balance at any time. They just assumed that meant it was simple interest that accrued but in reality, it was prepaid interest. The salesperson did not actually lie because they can pay off early, they just have to pay all of the interest when they do. Be wary and read everything.

Not reading debt settlement agreements allows debtors to go merrily on believing they are resolving all of their debt. This usually continues until they notice the balance on select debts has hardly been touched. Many of my clients find that they actually owe more than they did when they went to the debt settlement company in the first place. This is because the debt settlement company commission structure takes most of their commission up front before allocating much to your creditors. The debt settlement firms are protected because hidden in their stack of documents was a disclaimer that some debts will not be resolved as fast as others and may even increase in the interim.

A reputable debt settlement company will sit down with you and outline what they hope to accomplish with each of your creditors and will give you a timeline for accomplishing the goal. They will have a signed contract with each of your creditors. A contract you will have also signed, and they will freely give you copies of all documents. They will have amortization schedules for each debt showing how fast the debt will be paid and you should be able to monitor the progress each month. Unfortunately, as we have discussed, there are firms where you do not get that kind of attention. Those firms build a house of cards knowing that at some point it will all come crashing down. Of course, it won't fall until they get most if not all of their commission and of course, the stack of documents will make it clear it was all your fault.

The house of cards is just one of the potential pitfalls. There are a number of scenarios that you may want to avoid. If they are a reputable company, they will be up front with you. In reality, debt settlement is simply an attempt to put together a chapter 13 plan without the force of law. That is an important point. ***Without the force of law***. That is why it is extremely important there are enforceable written contracts.

Debt settlement companies will often not get anything in writing when they negotiate a settlement with a company. The "deal" the creditor may offer is that they will settle a $5,000.00 debt for a lower amount if you make 24 payments of $100.00 per month. The only catch is that they didn't or won't put that deal in writing.

If the company you have chosen to do your debt settlement for you says that a written agreement in not necessary, “we can trust them,” run as fast as you can. There is one truth about creditors, they can (and do) lie to you; unless you have a written agreement to prove that a deal exists, you lose. I often get clients seeking a bankruptcy when they near the last payment pursuant to the unwritten agreement, and they learn the creditor has had a change of heart and now wants the balance paid in full.

The second thing that I often see is that the client still end up in lawsuits. Remember, lawsuits are a real threat to your financial future. Many companies will tell their clients not to worry about a lawsuit that has been filed with the court and served. Clients are told, “don’t worry about it.” Unfortunately, all too often, they aren’t worried about it either and you might end up with a judgment. A lawsuit should be a clear indication that the debt settlement negotiations aren’t going very well and you need to find out what is going on. A reputable company is not afraid to tell you what is happening in your case. Hopefully, a lawsuit is not the first indication you get that things are not going well. You need to stay involved and monitor everything. Don't be afraid to ask questions.

These examples should be what all of us are doing. Read contracts, monitor performance, and ask questions. It doesn't matter what kind of contract it is. We are asked to sign documents all the time. Even I have to catch myself and read before I sign. It is sometimes to tempting to just trust that you are not being taken advantage of. Trust is good in a marriage but not so much in a business deal.

If we need a debt negotiation we should make sure everything is in writing. The next thing you have to worry about is any **tax implications** a negotiated settlement brings. When a debt is forgiven the amount forgiven becomes taxable income. Your creditor will send you a 1099-C-Cancellation of Debt. Often, clients finish the debt settlement plan only to find they have a huge tax debt. That should be an issue that is discussed up front before you agree to any plan. Not all cancelled debt becomes taxable income. Debts cancelled in bankruptcy are not taxable. Cancelled debts are not taxable income if you are insolvent. The IRS requires a Form 982 for either of those situations. The important part for you to understand is these issues should be discussed with you before you begin. If the attorney tells you he doesn't deal with the tax implications, you need another attorney.

This advice is not just for people in financial distress. It is good advice to avoid ever getting into financial distress. I cannot tell you the number of times I had clients come into my office because they were being garnished on a lawsuit they thought they had taken care of. They called the plaintiff and explained they were not the right people and believe it or not, sometimes they were right. The wrong people get sued all the time and there are other situations where the lawsuit is wrong.

My own mother had a student loan from decades ago and paid it off, but she did not keep the documents showing she paid it off. Decades after it was paid off her tax refund was garnished to pay the outstanding balance of the student loan. We had to file legal action to get the funds back. She was not sued because federal law allows for garnishment of tax refunds for student loans without having to file a lawsuit but there are many such examples where the creditor might file a lawsuit.

I had clients where the plaintiff sued the wrong person with the same or similar name, and I had clients who had already paid off a debt but could not prove it. Often the situation was exacerbated because the clients thought it was as simple as calling the plaintiff and explaining the situation. Often the plaintiff acted like they agreed and promised to dismiss the action and the client forgot all about it believing it had gone away.

Let me be blunt. **You can't trust anybody** else when it is your financial future on the line. The plaintiff simply continued the lawsuit and received a default judgment because there was no answer to the complaint. Does that mean you can't try to reason with a plaintiff? Of course not but do follow up. Check the courts records and if there is no record of a dismissal, don't miss the deadline to answer the complaint.

As an attorney I often just made a phone call to attempt to resolve legal actions. Most of an attorney's work is done by telephone but I also always asked for a copy of the motion to dismiss and order dismissing the case. I even went further and looked at the court docket to make sure it had in fact been dismissed and I printed out a copy of the order of dismissal. If I did not find the dismissal, I answered the complaint. I once had a divorce client whose case was settled by agreement of the parties and we submitted a stipulation and order to the court. Back then there was no internet so I actually had to get a copy of the order affixed with the courts stamp. Years went by before I was contacted by my client who said his ex-spouse had filed another divorce action because the one I filed was never completed. Sure enough, the settlement documents could not be located by the court but I had a copy with the courts stamp. I provided a copy of the documents and had them entered and then filed a motion to dismiss the current case.

If you ever face anything significant, make sure you follow through and keep copies of all documents settling a case. I always told my client to get certified copies. There are not a lot of real significant documents in our lives. We all keep our birth certificates, church records, and marriage certificates. Most of us even keep proof of paid off mortgages and cars. I believe you should also keep decrees of divorce, bank account opening documents, credit card opening documents, and other settlement documents from any type of legal action. It is important to keep opening documents for all open accounts if for no other reason than you can keep track of what accounts you have open. A shocking number of my clients had no idea what accounts they even had opened. Those type of documents will probably all fit in a small file folder.

Recap:

1. Keep all options on the table.
2. Read and understand contracts and agreements.
3. Stay involved and ask questions.
4. Remember tax implications.
5. Resolve issues
    a. Follow-up to make sure it is resolved.
    b. Never miss a deadline if it isn't resolved.
    c. Get and keep copies of the documents.

Chapter 3

Sometimes Bankruptcy Can't be Avoided

It should be undisputed; bankruptcy is not for everybody. Just like debt settlement companies that don't do anything but debt settlement, most firms that practice bankruptcy limit their practice to bankruptcy. Unfortunately, there are bankruptcy attorneys out there whose goal is to file a bankruptcy for every person who comes through the door. There are bankruptcy attorneys who only file chapter 7 cases and remarkably, every person that comes in the door is pigeon-holed into a chapter 7 case. Attorneys need a good working knowledge of bankruptcy law if they are going to file chapter 13 cases. The attorneys who only file chapter 7 cases generally do so because they don't have the required knowledge or experience to file anything else.

There are also attorneys who pigeonhole everyone who walks in the door into a chapter 13 case. They do so for a more nefarious reason. They have made a business decision to file chapter 13 cases simply because they make more money from chapter 13 cases. It will vary from state to state but generally Chapter 13 fees are about $3,000.00 more than chapter 7 fees. There is more work associated with a chapter 13 case but it is still quite a bit more lucrative for the attorney to file a chapter 13 case.

When you are choosing a bankruptcy attorney ask questions just so you can get a feel for whether they have a good knowledge of both chapter 7 and chapter 13 cases because they are interrelated. Occasionally, something happens where a chapter 13 case has to be converted to a chapter 7 and vice versa. Ask the attorney why one is better for you than the other. Remember, each one addresses different goals. For example, a chapter 13 case can cure a mortgage arrearage thereby allowing you to stop a foreclosure action so you can keep your home. A chapter 7 case does not resolve a mortgage arrearage. If you are facing foreclosure you will most likely lose the home in a chapter 7 case.

Occasionally, a strategy requires a unique action, and those kinds of cases require an attorney with a complete understanding of the bankruptcy code. An attorney who has a good understanding of the bankruptcy code invites your questions. My goal was to make sure I fully discussed and explained the bankruptcy options as well as other non-bankruptcy options that might be available to my clients. Anything short of that means an attorney hasn't done a very good job or worse, doesn't have your best interest in mind.

A good bankruptcy attorney knows the oddities of the bankruptcy code and how the law might affect the client. Unfortunately, the bankruptcy code is replete with sections that require a good working knowledge to understand. For that reason, it is also not wise to attempt bankruptcy on your own. That is not to say you can't file your bankruptcy pro se because the law allows anybody to represent themselves. Pro Se is Latin meaning "for yourself." A pro se person is one that represents him or herself without an attorney.

Before representing yourself remember the famous quote:

> *"He who will be his own Counsellor, shall be sure to have a fool for his client" (William De Britaine, Humane Prudence [1702]*

I point this out because all too often I see pro se debtors fail to do something the law requires and as a result have their case dismissed because they were not aware of one of the many hoops that Congress had created. The goal of bankruptcy is to receive a discharge of debts. A case that is dismissed does not proceed to that point and the debtor does not receive a discharge of their debts. It is as though they never filed in the first place, and they are back to square one.

It isn't just pro se clients who may not understand the bankruptcy law. I have had many clients who came to me to fix problems created by other attorneys. Unfortunately, at that point it ends up costing more to fix the problem than it would have to just do it right in the first place. Bankruptcy law is like no other legal area as it has its own code and procedure rules. You can assume if some attorneys don't fully understand bankruptcy that you may also have problems trying to do it yourself. If you need a bankruptcy, **hire a knowledgeable attorney**!

As a matter of fact, be careful with the attorney you retain. Make sure the attorney knows what he or she is doing. Unfortunately, bankruptcy is not easy to understand, even for many lawyers. I have faced many opposing attorneys who do not ordinarily practice bankruptcy law and often they argue the motion so poorly that bankruptcy judges have told me not to bother with a response and simply ruled against them. I was once placed in the uncomfortable position of having to file a motion for sanctions against another attorney. I had to do it because it was in my client's best interest. I wrote the following in a court filing that an attorney:

> *"has a persistent and disturbing pattern of this type of conduct with her bankruptcy cases. A search of the bankruptcy records found that she filed 28 bankruptcy cases*

> *between May 5, 2010, and January 13, 2011. Of those 28 cases, only 2 have received a discharge. In one of the two discharges, the discharge was obtained only after the Debtor filed a pro se Motion to Remove Counsel and Represent Myself, stating as grounds that there were "[c]ommunication problems, and court documents not filed when I was told otherwise by my counsel."*

While that was an egregious case, there are many examples of attorneys not understanding the law and their clients suffering because of their lack of understanding. Again, it is extremely important to ask questions and make sure you feel comfortable with the attorney's knowledge and communication. It won't take very long for an attorney who doesn't have a good working knowledge of the bankruptcy code to stumble, and you may or may not recognize it when it happens.

There are a few basic differences between chapter 7 and chapter 13 cases. There are certain situations where the bankruptcy code requires that a chapter 13 be filed. For example, the bankruptcy code requires that every debtor complete a means test. The point of the means test is to ensure that most people with over median-income can't file chapter 7 simply because they live above their means. The means test only allows so much for housing, vehicle, food, etc., based on the level of income and the number of people in the household. The amounts a debtor can claim for each is limited and so even if they have an expensive vehicle, they cannot deduct the amount they actually pay. They can only deduct a reasonable amount as defined by the local standards. Bankruptcy trustees and courts view the National and Local Standards outlined by the IRS to be the reasonable expenses that are allowed.

If it appears a reasonable lifestyle will leave income that can be paid to unsecured creditors, they may be required to file a chapter 13 and make a payment that will pay those unsecured creditors. Most debtors are not adversely affected by implementation of the means test as they are under the median income. A few, however, are over the median income and the means test then comes into play. Median income levels vary depending on where you live in the United States.

Most individuals file either chapter 7 or chapter 13 cases. There are other chapters, such as chapter 11 and chapter 12, that are infrequently used. Chapter 11 is usually for used by businesses and a chapter 12 is intended for farmers and fishermen. I will give a basic overview of each of the bankruptcy chapters that are available to individuals and couples.

Chapter 11

Chapter 11 is primarily designed for the rehabilitation of distressed businesses. It can also be used by individuals if their debts exceed the statutory limit set for chapter 13 cases. Chapter 11 cases are generally complex and very expensive. Even the most reasonable and least expensive attorney will require thousands of dollars as a retainer to start. There will likely be additional fees as the case progresses. Similar to chapter 12, the debtor becomes a "debtor-in-possession" and has to fulfill his statutory duties as he operates the business or family finances.

A trustee is not generally appointed unless some interested party asks the court to do so and shows sufficient "cause" such as fraud or mismanagement (on the part of the debtor-in-possession). A committee of unsecured creditors is usually appointed in Chapter 11 cases to monitor the debtor's progress. The Chapter 11 debtor's ultimate goal is to file a plan of reorganization that complies with the bankruptcy code and is accepted by the creditors and the court. Because of the complexity and cost, chapter 11 is rarely used by individuals.

Chapter 12

Chapter 12 was enacted into law in 1986 to provide relief for family farmers and fishermen with a regular income. Chapter 12 has characteristics of both Chapter 13 and Chapter 11. Individuals are eligible to file where aggregate debts do not exceed the maximum amount allowed by the code. This amount can change, A plan must be filed within 90 days of filing. That time limit can be extended by the court if there is good cause to do so. A trustee is appointed upon filing but the family farmer is the debtor-in-possession and operates the farm as long as it is done in a manner consistent with the bankruptcy code. After confirmation, payments are made to satisfy the terms of the plan.

Chapter 7

A chapter 7 is referred to as a liquidation case. A trustee is appointed when a chapter 7 is filed; his or her job is to find the debtor's non-exempt assets, liquidate them, and pay what is possible to the unsecured creditors. The trustee's job is to also make sure the debtor qualifies for a chapter 7. A vast majority of chapter 7 cases have nothing to liquidate and are referred to as no-asset cases. Understandably, everybody owns things that are non-exempt that a trustee could sell if he or she so chooses. But understand, the trustee is operating a business and making business decisions. If the value of the property is *DE MINIMIS*, the trustee won't sell it. De Minimis simply means lacking significance or importance or so minor as to merit disregard

To explain "de minimis," I often use what I call my Boise story as an explanation. Boise is 500 miles from where I live. Someone in Boise owes me $50.00; all I have to do to get my money is to drive up there. Unfortunately, it will cost me $60.00 in gas to do that. I am not going to drive to Boise for $50.00 any more than the trustee is going to sell your $100.00 computer. It costs him more time and effort to do so than it is worth. The exception to that logic is where there are a number of things worth $100.00 that add up to a point where it becomes worth it. Rarely, however, is that the case.

The bankruptcy code also allows states to enact their own exemptions, so exemptions vary from state to state.

An exemption is what you get to keep when you file a bankruptcy.

You may remember O. J. Simpson moved to Florida to avoid having to pay the civil judgment that the California courts ordered him to pay to the victim's families. It is assumed he did that because California had a limit on the amount of equity in a house that was exempt while there was a more favorable exemption limit in Florida. Well-off individuals often relocate to a jurisdiction that allows them to retain more of their wealth.

Congress took steps to curb the incentive for forum shopping with a law change that occurred in 2005. Exemptions used to simply be the ones that existed in the state in which one lived when the bankruptcy was filed. Under the 2005 code change, an individual has to use the state exemption where the "*debtor's domicile has been located for the 730 days immediately preceding the date of the filing of the petition or if the debtor's domicile has not been located in a single State for such 730-day period, the place in which the debtor's domicile was located for 180 days immediately preceding the 730-day period or for a longer portion of such 180-day period than in any other place.*" Forum shopping is now more of a preparatory move rather than a reactionary move because the law change. Unfortunately, the bankruptcy code that was passed in 2005 has many sections that are just as crazy. Many sections are written such that the fix may actually be worse than the original problem.

Chapter 13

A chapter 13 is referred to as a wage earner plan and is used by individuals with a regular source of income to pay their debts consistent with the bankruptcy code. Chapter 13 is used when a chapter 7 does not accomplish your goals. Generally, a chapter 13 is used to cure mortgage arrearage in order to retain your home, to protect and retain assets that could have been taken in a chapter 7, to avoid large penalties and the accrual of interest on priority and non-dischargeable debts, to take advantage of the cram down provisions of chapter 13, or to strip off a 2nd or 3rd mortgage. With home prices increasing so rapidly it is becoming almost impossible to strip a 2nd mortgage because in order to strip a 2nd mortgage the loan has to be wholly unsecured. In other words, the home value is less than what is owed to the first mortgage. Most people believe that a chapter 13 simply reorganizes debt and all debt has to be paid for through payment made to a trustee. Most chapter 13 cases, however, do not pay much, if anything, to unsecured creditors.

The bankruptcy code outlines three ways to evaluate how much has to be paid to unsecured creditors. The first two are part of the good faith test. The first part of the good faith test is the means test. If a debtor has income that is over the median income, the means test has to be completed and if there is excess income according to the means test, the excess income has to be paid to unsecured creditors. Income for the means test is determined by adding all of the household income that has been received in the last 6 full months and then dividing the total by six. The bankruptcy code does not define a household but it is widely accepted that a household does not include roommates, but it does generally include a roommate who is largely treated as a spouse. The month of the filing does not count in that calculation.

For example, if one was to file on November 29th, the full 6 month period would be May 1 through October 31. Deductions on the means test are a combination of amounts that the IRS says a person with the stated income and family size should be spending as well as a component for secured and priority debt that actually must be paid.

The bankruptcy code requires that all of the "excess" income must be paid to unsecured creditors through a chapter 13 plan. Debtors must propose to pay the excess income times 60 to unsecured creditors. The reason for the 60 months is because a plan has to be a minimum of 36 months and a maximum of 60 months. Over income debtors are required to pay for 60 months.

The other element of the good faith test is that unsecured creditors must be paid as much in a chapter 13 case as they would have received if a chapter 7 case had been filed and there were non-exempt assets the trustee could have liquidated. This is called the liquidation analysis.

A secured creditor is paid depending on how you choose to address them. Secured property can either be retained or surrendered through the plan. Secured debt can often be lowered and paid at the fair market value existing at the time of the bankruptcy filing. This means that if you owe $20,000.00 on a vehicle that is only worth $10,000.00, you pay $10,000.00 as a secured claim and the balance is paid as an unsecured claim. The benefit is that the secured portion is paid at 100% with a small interest rate while the unsecured portion will receive very little to nothing depending on how much is required pursuant to the means and good faith tests.

This is called a cram down and it is allowed by the bankruptcy code whenever you have a vehicle that was purchased more than 910 days before the filing of the bankruptcy or when you have other secured property that was purchased more than a year before the filing of the bankruptcy. Mortgage loans on your primary residence cannot be crammed down. A wholly unsecured 2nd or 3rd mortgage lien, however, can be "stripped off." A lien that is stripped off becomes an unsecured claim and is paid just like other unsecured claims.

There are statutory debt limits in a chapter 13 case. When I was practicing an individual could file only if their unsecured debts did not exceed approximately $336,900.00 and their secured debts did not exceed approximately $1,010,650.00. The amount of allowed debt changes from time to time but will remain close to those amounts. You will have to check to see what the current debt limits are.

It is important to have a basic knowledge of bankruptcy when that may be an option. Frankly, even if you are not ready to file bankruptcy but it may be an option in the future you should talk to an attorney. Unfortunately, there are many mistakes debtors make that end up harming them more than helping. We will discuss a few of those problems in the next chapter. This chapter provides the bare minimum you should know about bankruptcy.

Hopefully, you now have enough knowledge that when you sit down with an attorney you will be able to spot whether an attorney knows bankruptcy, or he or she is just giving you a well-rehearsed sales pitch. There are so many attorneys who will simply tell you what they think you want to hear knowing they cannot actually accomplish what they are promising. All they want is to get you to sign on the bottom line of a retainer agreement. They will break the bad news to you later.

We saw that earlier with the attorney who was willing to file a motion to refinance knowing it would never be approved. Of course, I am not suggesting you get an attorney who won't try to accomplish your goals if they are reasonably attainable. I actually loved a good fight in court but there are some things that clearly cannot happen.

Filing a motion to refinance that is clearly not in the client's best interest and filing a bankruptcy where the debtor is clearly not eligible are two such examples we have already shown.

We have peripherally shown other examples such as the client who wanted to file a chapter 13 even though a chapter 7 would accomplish all of their goals. I wouldn't expect the short bankruptcy section of this book to give you everything you need to know to avoid the shyster bankruptcy attorney who just wants you to sign on the bottom line but going into a bankruptcy office with an open mind and talking to more than one bankruptcy attorney is a good idea. Have them explain their proposed action and why it will work for you and then research each option before going back to either attorney.

Let me provide an example where you have the ability to check an attorney's advice. I have had clients come to my office wanting a file a chapter 13 bankruptcy even though they had debts that were clearly over the statutory limit. Remember, one of the things about a chapter 13 bankruptcy is there are statutory limits on how much you can owe. They had been to an attorney who was not aware of the actual statutory limit and told them they could file.

I have also had clients come to my office where an attorney told them they could not file because they were over the statutory limit. The limit, however, had just recently been adjusted and the adjustment made them eligible to file a chapter 13. Frankly, that is an easy issue to research even for a non-attorney. Do an internet search on statutory limits for chapter 13. I was always amazed when I saw cases from other firms where the attorney either did not understand the statutory limit or simply did not bother to check.

That is an obvious example where a little knowledge helps you choose the right attorney. If an attorney does not know what the statutory limit is then they probably aren't the attorney you want. That is one of the bankruptcy basics. As I pointed out earlier, I never objected to a potential client getting a second opinion or doing a little research and neither should any other attorney. Potential more often than not generally came back to me anyway.

It is important for you to understand this is not legal advice and I am not advising how to proceed with your situation. What I am doing is advising you to seek quality legal counsel and be prepared to evaluate their advice so you can avoid the shyster attorney. For advice about your individual situation, you **should** obtain legal advice from a competent local attorney.

Recap:

1. Hire a knowledgeable attorney;
2. Have basic knowledge of bankruptcy before you talk to an attorney.

.

Chapter 4

Mistakes People Make

There are some basic things all people should know. Healthy finances depend on avoiding mistakes that will set back goals or cause financial failure. Sometimes financial mistakes are made with the best of intentions simply because of not understanding what the repercussions of certain actions are. There are two parts of healthy finances that are necessary to understand.

The first is to understand and protect the assets that have already been accumulated. The second; Explore income improvement and then make a plan. Do not make mistakes that cause more harm than good and it is often difficult to determine where that fine line is. Understanding that fine line helps in making wise decisions.

Understanding and Protecting Assets

Protecting your assets is a very important part of the picture. Often, you might not think of a 401k as an asset, but it is. It is an asset you are building to make sure you have sufficient resources for retirement. It goes without saying that social security is woefully insufficient to maintain the lifestyle you presently have. There are unique rules you have to follow with 401k plans. The first is that you are not permitted to withdraw funds from a 401k without having to pay a hefty penalty. I saw far too many clients who had healthy 401k retirement plans and they took funds from them in hopes of saving themselves from a financial crisis. Sometimes that might be the answer, but more often, it is not.

Early withdrawal of funds from a 401k is very expensive. Usually, the funds from a 401k come from two sources. Most is money that you earn and is invested in a 401k pre-tax. In other words, the money you put into the 401k has not been taxed. The second part of a 401k is the amount your employer contributes to the plan. That is usually referred to as matching funds. Those funds are also un-taxed.

Once you withdraw funds from a 401k, you

have to pay taxes on withdrawn funds. Because of these tax implications, that is an expensive way to get immediate funds. Not only are you paying taxes on the amount withdrawn, you may also have to pay a higher tax on all of your income because the additional taxable income puts you in a higher tax bracket.

For instance, suppose you are single and have a taxable income of $36,000 per year and you withdraw $6,000 giving you a taxable income of $42,000. Currently, a taxpayer pays 12% tax on income up to $41,775. When your taxable income goes above that amount it jumps to a 22% tax rate. You could be paying 22% on all of your income instead of 12%. The extra 10% is approximately $3,600 more in taxes. The tax system is never that simple because there are several factors involved and some adjustments because of the way the funds may have been spent but universally there is still going to some incremental increase in taxable income. And as always, tax rates may change but almost always, the rate increases making it even worse.

Withdrawals from a 401k also causes another financial hit. A withdrawal prior to a certain age means you have to pay an **early withdrawal** penalty. The early withdrawal penalty is currently ten percent but as with most things, taxes and penalties can increase. You will end up having to pay a $600 penalty on the $6,000 withdrawal.

Withdrawn funds:	$6,000.00
22% tax on withdrawn funds	-1,320.00
Extra 10% tax on all other income	-3,600.00
10% penalty on withdrawn funds	- 600.00
Actual funds to you	$ 480.00

The actual increase to you from your $6,000 withdrawal could be as low as $480.00 and that does not make any sense. It will seem much better than that at first because much of the tax will not be paid until tax time. Of course that is a worst case scenario but the actual amount you receive will be drastically less than $6,000. You may be lucky and your income together with the withdrawn funds may not take you into another tax bracket. Hopefully, you won't rely on dumb luck, and you will have calculated the costs beforehand. Even in the best case, you still end up with only $4,080, just slightly two-thirds of the amount taken and that may or may not make sense in the long run.

The lesson is that you should run a few calculations before actually taking any funds from your 401k. If you find you are in the group where it takes you into a higher tax bracket it may make no sense taking out 401k funds. Also, keep in mind there are also state taxes and, in some locations, there might even be local taxes.

I always advised my clients that they should count on about forty percent of the funds they withdraw going to the government as taxes and early withdrawal penalty. That means if you need $10,000 to deal with your financial crisis you will need to withdraw about $16,666 from your account and that is if the withdrawal does not take you into a higher tax bracket. I can not emphasize this enough. You don't have to guess it is only 40%. You can and should run a calculation which will provide you a much better idea of the spendable amount you will receive.

As a bankruptcy attorney the biggest problem I saw was people who had withdrawn funds only to be surprised they had to pay taxes on those funds and maybe even an increased amount on all of their other income if it took them into a higher tax bracket. Most often they found themselves in my office when they realized the withdrawal wasn't enough to resolve the debt crisis. A secondary reason was they did not plan for the taxes and had already spent the money and they needed a bankruptcy to address the outstanding taxes. Someone with $25,000 in debts they are struggling to pay back takes a withdrawal of $25,000, this is not enough to pay the $25K in debts. In order to pay the entire amount, they could actually need approximately $41,666 and again, that does not include any additional taxes because of the withdrawal potentially taking them into a higher tax bracket. Twenty percent will be automatically deducted for the potential tax ramifications before you even receive any funds but that is rarely enough. While the federal taxes are usually withheld before you see the money, state taxes are not, even though you will have to pay taxes in most states. Twenty percent is also often not enough to even pay the entire amount of federal taxes.

When all is said and done people generally are still in trouble because of poor planning. People want to avoid bankruptcy if at all possible, so they withdrew funds only to find out they still need to file bankruptcy. Please don't make those mistakes. If I could have advised them before they withdrew funds, I would have told them about the tax issue, the penalty, and the state taxes. If they still wanted to withdraw funds I would advise them to do so only if they KNEW they would be able to avoid bankruptcy by taking an early withdrawal.

In most states, a 401k account is an exempt asset that your creditors cannot touch even if they have a judgment. The bankruptcy code specifically exempts a 401k. In legal words, a 401k is exempt from execution. That means a 401k cannot be taken by a creditor through a legal process nor would you lose it in a bankruptcy. However, that does not stop creditors from threatening to go after your retirement account unless you agree to use it to pay at least some of the debt with 401k funds. That way they get exempt assets from you before you are forced to file a bankruptcy. Do not be fooled by their threats. The 401k is yours to keep for your retirement. Do not be bullied!

In most states houses, or at least some equity in houses, are also exempt. Many lenders will “offer” to allow you additional time to make payment on a debt if only you will guarantee the new payment plan using your home as collateral. Creditors often will also restart loan payments with a “slight” interest increase as long as you will pledge any exempt as collateral. Both, however, are just tricks to get you to pledge an exempt asset. Remember, as nice as they sound, they are not trying to help you.

These are assets they would not otherwise

be able to get to in a legal proceeding. The only time a creditor can get to an exempt asset is when an exempt asset is **voluntarily pledged** as security. No matter how sincere they sound they aren't really trying to help you. They are just trying to wiggle their way into getting your exempt assets. Don't fall for those collection tricks.

Think before you act. Ask yourself, what makes you think you can make a payment now when you couldn't before? Sometimes you can and sometimes you can't. Unless you can look at some tangible reason you can, don't risk it. You are likely just putting off the inevitable and in so doing might also lose exempt assets in the process; it is a risky gamble. One of the hardest things I had to do as an attorney is tell people it was time to cut losses and start over. I always preferred to do that when I could temper it with the news that they would not lose a 401k, homes, and cars. Talk to an attorney before you risk everything you own.

As discussed, it isn't just 401k accounts that are exempt. Every state has exempt assets.

Voluntarily pledging exempt assets isn't the only way to lose everything. There are times when I have seen people sell exempt assets in the hopes of avoiding bankruptcy. Sometimes that might work but often there is another solution. Unfortunately, sometimes it is just time to just start over and that may mean a bankruptcy. Perhaps it means taking a combination of actions that allow you to avoid bankruptcy. Talk to an attorney to see what your viable options might be.

For example, I had a case where the clients owed approximately $45,000 in debt and had $60,000 in home equity. If they filed a chapter 7 bankruptcy, they would lose their home and for one reason or another they could not file a chapter 13 bankruptcy. They would, however, still get paid the amount of the homestead exemption. A local attorney can tell you what the homestead exemption is in your state as it is not the same in every state.

In this case the chapter 7 trustee would sell the home and use the funds to pay off the mortgage and then use the rest of the funds above the homestead exemption to pay creditors and pay his own fees.

Miraculously, the home is sold on a fast sale where all the funds in excess of the homestead exemption are eaten up in payments to creditors and the trustee costs and fees. Rather than just filing a bankruptcy for a potential client, I gave them the option of selling their home themselves and using the funds to make debt settlement deals with their creditors.

The selling point to their creditors was always that the trustee costs and fees would invariably eat into what they would be paid because trustee fees and costs always come out first before paying any creditor. We generally had one year from the sale date because the funds from a home sale retain their character as homestead funds for that long and creditors usually did not dare try to get to them because that would trigger an automatic bankruptcy and they would get even less.

My fees somehow were always much lower

than what the trustee costs and fees would have been and unlike when a trustee sells a home in a fire sale, the clients had the opportunity to sell their home for a fair market value. In the end, they avoided bankruptcy and walked away with some money. Of course, in the state where I practiced, they could have simply filed a bankruptcy and if the trustee took the home and sold it, he would have had to pay them the exemption amount of $40,000.

As it was, they only received about $25,000 by selling the home on their own and then having us negotiate debt settlement. We will discuss quantifying everything a little later. I always advised clients to quantify every factor and in this case the loss of $15,000 was a cost they were willing to absorb in order to avoid having a bankruptcy on their record. In other words, the avoidance of a bankruptcy was worth $15,000 to them. That path is not necessarily for everybody, but it is an option you should at least know about. If you go to a firm that only does bankruptcy it is an option you will likely never hear about.

I said earlier I did not necessarily like debt settlement. What I should have said is debt settlement rarely worked once people "got desperate enough" to seek legal advice. A debt settlement may have worked before the situation became desperate. Often people simply have no idea what to do so they become paralyzed and do nothing while the situation becomes worse with additional interest and penalties. It does not take long for a $5000 debt to double from interest and penalties.

It may have been a good idea to do a debt negotiation with funds from a 401k or sale of a home before bankruptcy becomes inevitable. Every so often we could still avoid a bankruptcy but generally, waiting too long to find out what your options are precludes you from being able to take advantage of options that may have once been available. The point is people wait far too long before seeking advice from an attorney. They need advice when they first start seeing trouble on the horizon. A small consultation fee may be far less expensive than the mistakes made without the consultation. In this day and age many attorneys will offer a free consultation in which you will receive enough information to be able to decide if an attorney's services are needed. Talking to more than one gives you an even better idea of the direction to take.

Let's take a minute to discuss finances even when bankruptcy is not on the horizon. Seeking advice from an attorney whenever making major financial decisions is not a bad idea. For instance, I once had a client who had been approached by a man with a proposal that she buy his $50,000 vehicle so she could drive for an app-based ride share business. As an attorney I immediately saw a few red flags. The first was why did it have to be a $50,000 vehicle. His explanation was that she would need to be able to carry a number of passengers as well as skis. The second was that at the time local governments were not yet sold on the idea and were contemplating passing laws that did not allow those type of businesses. Local governments did not want them competing with taxis who had been given a limited number of permits to operate.

I explained my concerns to the client and told her that if she really wanted to do that she should get the seller to concede there would be no deficiency balance in the event the vehicle was repossessed or voluntarily surrendered and that he would make no negative credit reports in the event of late payments or either occurred. The seller was insistent this was a great idea and convinced her he should discuss the idea with me. After his pitch to me I simply told him we were not opposed if he would also assume some of the risk by agreeing to those terms.

He was so convinced it would work he agreed to the terms, and she purchased the vehicle. She drove the vehicle for a few months before the city passed an ordinance making it almost impossible for such a business to survive. It took legal action against the city for them to relent but in the meantime, people struggled to stay afloat. It became impossible for her to keep the vehicle and she voluntarily surrendered the vehicle. She was grateful we included those terms. My modest fees were well worth every penny. She walked away still financially intact.

For those experiencing financial distress, it is important to understand what is exempt in your locale. Each state's laws outline their exemptions and every state is different. An attorney consult can go over your assets and help you understand if they are exempt in your state and advise you on how to proceed.

Social Security is an exempt asset in most circumstances. The federal Social Security Act exempts social security up to $2,500. The amount may periodically change so it is important to check. If you have a judgment creditor that is threatening to garnish your social security if you don't agree to make a monthly payment, and you understand that social security is exempt, you will know that you can laugh at the collector that is making the hollow threat. That doesn't mean that you have no worries, but you don't need to worry about the social security being taken. To protect the social security, you might need to make a few changes about how you handle your money. I always advised my clients on social security to maintain a separate account for social security, so it is not comingled with other funds. That way there can be no confusion as to whether or not it is social security.

Any firm that practices in the area of finance and bankruptcy should also be able to discuss asset protection. Any time you are facing a financial crisis you should have enough information to know what assets are and are not at risk. In other words, what assets do you need to protect from collection? There are several situations where you just can't do anything at the moment to address your debts. One such example is when you are not eligible for a chapter 13 because you exceed the debt limit, but you still want to protect your assets. Sometimes asset protection combined with strategies to lower your debt below the debt limit work to get a client to the point they can do a chapter 13 allowing them to keep their assets and address their bills.

I have had clients where we had to negotiate a surrender of a secured asset because they had too much secured debt to qualify for a chapter 13 and once we accomplished that we could then proceed with a chapter 13. We won't go into asset protection in depth here but suffice it to say there are a number of simple strategies that can be taken to make it much more difficult for creditors to get to your assets. The main point is know what is at risk and learn how to protect those assets.

As already discussed, one of the assets that is not generally at risk is social security benefits. Many courts have said if you can "track" your social security, it is still protected. For example, if you have a bank account that you only use for social security and no other funds ever go into that account, the mere fact that it is in a bank account does not mean that it loses its characteristic as social security up to the limit allowed by the federal Social Security Act. On the other hand, if you comingle funds, then it is not so clear it is social security and creditors may attempt to garnish your bank account. Even if they are ultimately unsuccessful the funds can be frozen while it is being sorted out.

Funds are comingled if you put social security and your paycheck from a part time employment in the same account. That is the simplest form of asset protection. Simply set up a separate account for social security. You need to check with a local attorney to make sure that works in your jurisdiction. There are many ways to protect your assets while you are trying to carry out your plan to rejuvenate your financial future. An attorney can help you understand what needs to be done.

The second mistake many people make is to refinance away the equity they have in their home. Again, all states have an exemption for equity you may have in your home. The amounts, however, differ from state to state. Don't refinance with the ***hope*** that it will help you out of your financial distress. That is not to say that you can't or shouldn't use your equity to gain financial freedom. I see far too many people who have refinanced in the hopes of avoiding bankruptcy and then find that it just wasn't enough, and they still have to file the bankruptcy. Using exempt equity to secure a refinance is often not the best idea. This is no different than taking exempt money from a 401k hoping to solve financial problems. The only time you do either is if you **know** your financial distress will be resolved.

Generally, when people are considering using exempt assets to solve financial problems, they are attempting to avoid bankruptcy even if they don't fully understand bankruptcy is or may become an option. Sometimes it is wise to use your assets to avoid financial disaster and sometimes it is not wise. Again, discuss financial issues with a competent attorney.

As touched upon earlier, I often tell my clients that I want them to identify all of the issues that are important to them and then quantify them. Once quantified, make a cost benefit analysis. What are you willing to give up to avoid having to file a bankruptcy? If that number is $10,000.00, then put that amount as a cost of avoiding a bankruptcy. Likewise, what are you willing to pay to keep your house. Your desire to keep a house has a value. What is it? A person who cares highly about their house may take one step while a person who doesn't care about their home may pursue another course of action.

I once had a client who essentially only had one problem. She had a few other small debts but her main problem was she was behind on her house payment. Often, one of the things an attorney does is take emotion out of the situation and decisions are simply based on law and a cost/benefit analysis. I eventually learned that may not always be the best because I was not quantifying their feelings. After discussing my client's situation with her it was obvious, her best course of action was to file a chapter 7 and surrender her home as she was way upside down in the home. Ther only way of saving the home was to pay more money than the home was worth.

My advice to her was to simply surrender

the home and that it made no sense to do anything else. She burst into tears. Not just tears but hysterical uncontrollable bawling. It took her about 10 minutes to calm down enough to be able to discuss the issue. That is when she explained how devastating it would be for her to lose her home. Her family believed in home births. They even had a designated birthing room in the home.

All of her children had been born in that room. Her mother and all of her siblings had been born in that room and her grandmother and a few of her siblings had been born in that room. That was a real lesson to me. It was also a lessen to her. Her desire to keep that house had a value and she needed to quantify the value. In this case, the value was extremely high. We ended up doing a chapter 13 bankruptcy because that allowed her to save her home. That would not have been the decision for a person who didn't really have an emotional connection to the home and didn't care one way or the other.

Just as there may be a difference in a desire

to keep a home, I have some clients who would pay anything to avoid filing a bankruptcy and other clients who say there is nothing they would pay to avoid a bankruptcy. Both should quantify their desire to avoid or not avoid a bankruptcy.

Somewhere in the process the value becomes obvious and a client can regret not placing a value on actions and feelings. The lack of quantification sometimes leads people to regret what they have done. Eventually they realize they would have paid a great deal for their feelings and that would have led them to take another course of action. Sometimes they realize they really were not that attached and have taken too costly of action.

Obviously, you cannot pay any amount if you don't have that amount to pay. You do not sit down one day and quantify everything. It takes a great deal of thought. Once you have come up with numbers or find you don't have enough information to come up with a number, it is time to sit down with your attorney. A good attorney will be able to discuss the issues with you, so you have a better idea of how to quantify an issue. He or she will also be able to help you put together a realistic plan. Unfortunately, and this was part of my job that I hated, an attorney sometimes has to tell a client they simply do not have the ability to accommodate their quantified feelings.

Improve your income

It seems obvious that improving your income will help you rejuvenate your financial future. Nevertheless, it is worth discussing. We often don't move up and receive promotions for the same reason our finances have controlled us in the past rather than us controlling our finances. We wander aimlessly forced into being reactive rather than being proactive. We fail to plan for our employment future and just assume that we will receive promotions when our supervisors see that we are ready for them. We can accomplish so much more when we plan for our future and proactively look for and seek upward mobility.

My family moved to Utah when my father

was laid off from the railroad in Ohio. The only employment he could find was working with a neighbor in a potato cellar. Yes, we were just over the border from Idaho where they are famous for potatoes. He might have remained there for the rest of his working days if that had been his goal, but it was not.

Another example: Orison Swett Marden was born in Thornton Gore, New Hampshire. His mother died when he was three years old and his father, a farmer, hunter, and trapper, died when he was seven years old. Orison was forced to work as a "hired boy" to earn his keep. He could have remained a "hired boy" the rest of his life. Instead, he wrote:

> *We lift ourselves by our thought, we climb upon our vision of ourselves. If you want to enlarge your life, you must first enlarge your thought of it and of yourself. Hold the ideal of yourself as you long to be, always, everywhere - your ideal of what you long to attain - the ideal of health, efficiency, success.*

We need to do the same thing. What we think of ourselves does matter. Envision our future and then set a plan in motion to get there. Also, be realistic but don't sell yourself short. If everybody sold themselves short, we would have nobody who was the first person in their family line to get a college degree, buy a home, or start a business. They had to envision what nobody before them, at least not in their family, had done.

How do we set a plan in motion? First, decide what you want to do for a career. It doesn't matter what it is if it is sufficient to meet your needs and desires in life. Preferably you will choose a career that you enjoy doing. It doesn't matter what you want to do except you have to be happy doing it. Daniel Boone said "all you need for happiness is a good gun, a good horse, and a good wife." Well, alright, that doesn't help us today, but I really chuckle when I read it. Nevertheless, that was appropriate for his time, and it was what made him happy. A more appropriate quote was by Confucius.

"Choose a job you love and you will

never have to work a day in your life."

Granted, we can't all start our working days at the place we aspire to achieve but we can still take steps to get there. For example, some companies have a company university for their employees. The employees can take classes that will help in their career. Not everybody, however, works for such a company although on-the-job education is becoming a more prevalent model.

There are many ways to get training and knowledge that will help to achieve your goals. Most school districts have community education classes. Granted, the classes do not lead to an advances degree but you could get enough knowledge and training that you will be noticed by your employer. For example, a program support specialist might be involved with programs where there is a significant amount of computer programming. As the employee goes about doing the job, the supervisor or programmer may notice that his or her knowledge level is beyond the job they are currently doing and may become his or her mentor. You could also actively seek out a mentor.

To be succinct, as you take an interest in moving forward, others may also take an interest in helping you move forward. A good company will encourage employees to move up because it often translates into a better product; these same companies also often have programs to encourage and reimburse costs for attendance at post-secondary institutions. Why should you have any less faith in yourself than your company has in you! Go after your dream job!

Make a Plan--You Know the Options

You know about budgets, debt settlement, bankruptcy and several other issues already presented. Now it is time to put a plan together. You can't go on like you have in the past wandering aimlessly. You know where that leads you. A very bright anonymous person said:

> "If you do what you always did,
> you'll get what you always got."

It is time to put together a new plan. If you are just starting out, start with an original plan with goals in mind. Also, understand that plans always need to evolve and adjust. When I started college, I wanted to be an engineer. One engineering class and I was convinced my plan was not well thought out. Engineering was not for me. I finished my degree in economics and started on a path towards graduate school. I decided to get an MBA and applied to schools all over the country.

I was admitted to Mankato State, Boise State University, and provisionally to the University of Hawaii. I sent in the application to Hawaii but was still working on the letters of recommendation when my wife and I decided Hawaii would be too expensive, so I never sent in the recommendations. I even had them to send in because every school wanted recommendations. I have often regretted that decision. Not because it was a bad decision but because it sure would have been fantastic to live in Hawaii for a few years but that goes back to the realistic plans. It was just too expensive to be realistic.

I decided to go to Boise State University because it was only a one-year program. I paid the required 10% deposit on the tuition and applied for housing. We were a few days from loading up a U-Haul and moving to Idaho when a religious leader came to visit us. He asked me if I had any choice in the world of careers what would I be; I told him I would be an attorney. I had always wanted to be an attorney. I explained that an MBA was a fall back because my wife had been working so long to put me through school that I owed it to her to take the fastest course. His response shocked both my wife and me. He said it would be better for our family if I didn't settle for my second choice. My wife could continue working and we could figure it out. Our plan changed. Plans have to be well thought out and my original plan was not well thought out.

We cancelled the U-Haul, backed out of the housing, begrudgingly realized the tuition deposit was lost and two days later I walked into the LSAT exam without having had the opportunity to even study for the test. I did not do extremely well but for a non-academic who didn't study I did well enough to get into law school. I wish I had spoken to my religious leader before I made the plan to go to MBA school. That is another lesson for us. Don't be afraid to talk to trusted contacts about your plans.

Don't just plan to get out of debt, plan how you are going to get out of debt. Go further than just your debts. Your employment goals should be part of that plan. What do you want to accomplish after you get out of debt? Financially, the first step is to put together a budget. Remember, you need knowledge and information before you decide on a course of action. Don't limit knowledge and information to just financial matters. As you have successes in all aspects of your life you will increase your chance of also having financial success. Maybe I should have obtained some knowledge about engineering before I decided on that area of study. I could have asked engineers what their educational program was like. How much math do they need? That never even crossed my mind and I hate math. Get information before finalizing a plan.

Walt Disney once said "if you can dream it, you can do it." Dreaming sounds like it is a little too far-fetched when you are making a plan for your financial future. One should never base their financial future on dreams. However, a dream can serve as a path for setting goals Remember that not all dreams are viable or realistic as goals. One of my favorite dreams is that I win a $300 million lottery. That is a great dream but hardly a good foundation to base my goals upon.

I have other dreams, however. I dream that my children will grow up and be able to go to college and obtain a good education so they can have a good career and the ability to be financially vibrant. While I encourage them, I have to remember that it is my dream and they may have other ideas. That is great as long as their ideas also leads to being financially vibrant. I dream that one day I will be able to go to bed at night without having to worry about where the money is coming from to pay the bills. Both are fine dreams, and both are achievable. In order to achieve them, however, I have to put together a plan that gets me there. Rarely do things work out when there is no plan. Plan to get out of debt and stay out of debt.

It is always good to keep a sense of humor. When I think about dreaming, it reminds me of an old joke:

There was a man who prayed: "Dear God, please help me to win the lottery! Please, God, please! Help me to win the lottery."

The next day: "Dear God, please help me to win the lottery! Please, God, please! Help me to win the lottery!"

And, the next day and the next: "Dear God, please help me to win the lottery! Please, God, please! Help me to win the lottery."

Finally, one day as he was praying he heard a voice saying: "Dear Son, please! Please, Son, please! Buy a lottery ticket!"

Often, we approach a professional just like the man approached God: completely unprepared and without doing anything. Be prepared with more than a dream. As hard as I try, I can't help you win the lottery even if you buy a ticket. There is, however, a difference between dreaming and envisioning. Dorothea Brande, a writer, wrote:

"Envisioning the end is enough to put the means in motion"

It is a good idea to seek help once you understand the options that are available. Take some time to envision the end. What do you want? We would all love to win the lottery but what do you *realistically* want? When you stop to think about it, you can determine what you really want, what is realistic.

Some options have been presented in previous chapters. Now is the time to sit down and do a little preparation on order to put together a plan. Plans are forward-looking; plans give us motivation to do something. Without then, we are often paralyzed or at the very least, rudderless. I have helped thousands of clients, but I find the ones who have the most success are the ones that are involved and participate in crafting the solution.

Unfortunately, all too often I lament that I care about somebody's case more than they care about their own case. They simply haven't thought about what their goals are and how they can achieve that goal. They let life control them rather than them controlling life. Consequently, they feel paralyzed. If you haven't taken the opportunity to think about your dreams and determined which of your dreams are possible, you can't envision reaching them. As hard as I try, I can't envision any way of winning the lottery without buying a lottery ticket. However, the mere act of buying a lottery ticket leaves me more hopeless as each losing week passes.

On the other hand, I can envision paying off my credit cards. I just have to put a plan together that is realistic. At one point, I personally owed American Express over $60,000.00. I put together a plan to pay that off and then went to work implementing the plan. I knew I could not keep up with the interest so I called American Express and convinced them that if they waived interest for one-year I would be able to then pay off the balance and they would get all of their money back with some interest. Since I was a bankruptcy attorney, I also mentioned that if we could not come up with a solution that worked for both of us I would have no choice but to file for bankruptcy. As each month passed, I saw the plan working and as each month passed, I was more encouraged. But I couldn't have even started if I couldn't envision what I was going to do and how to do it. You are no different.

Put together a budget. Figure out what resources you do have. We all have some resources. The question that a good lawyer can help you determine is: What course of action is the best course of action based upon the resources that you have? For example, it doesn't do any good to try debt settlement negotiations if you don't have the resources to culminate a settlement.

An attorney who does debt settlement will be able to help you decide if a debt settlement is possible or if it will just be spinning your wheels. I like to go over the options with my clients, so they know the process, the goal and the potential for success. It is conceivable that one will want to attempt debt settlement knowing they are right on the edge of having enough resources to make it work. If it works, then they are thrilled, if it doesn't work, then they may have to shift directions. A good lawyer will let you know the ramifications of trying to make any plan work.

Recap:

1. Protect your exempt assets;
    a. 401k
    b. House
    c. Car
    d. Other assets
2. Improve your income
3. Make a Plan
    a. Think it through/talk to trusted contacts.
    b. Keep it a little flexible, plans can change

Chapter 5

Tips to Help You Rebuild Your Credit

There are many ways to rebuild your credit. To do so requires understanding what lenders look at when determining if you are creditworthy. Your creditworthiness is not determined by any one factor. There is so much written these days about credit score that many people believe the credit score is the only factor lenders look at. If that were true, there would be no need to complete an application for credit. A lender would simply use your social security number and get a credit report with your credit score. An application is important to lenders because they want to be able to calculate your debt-to-income ratio and debt-to-asset ratio.

To calculate your debt-to-income ratio, add up your fixed monthly expenses such as your car payments, minimum credit card payments, monthly child support, student loans, rent or mortgage, homeowner's insurance and property taxes. Some expensed don't appear to be fixed. For example, automobile expenses are not generally the same each month. Some months we have maintenance, some months have repairs, and sometimes we drive more than usual. You can look at those expenses as fixed by simply adding the previous year expenses and divide by 12. You could even get a more accurate number if you use a two-year average.

Every budget also needs a miscellaneous category. We all have spending that really doesn't fit in any category. They are miscellaneous expenses, and they won't go away. As strange as it sounds many people manage to put together a generous budget but only because they ignore several expenses. Travel to a wedding or a funeral may be a miscellaneous expense, but people often say that was only a one-time expense, so they just ignore them. While we may not have another wedding or funeral, we also may, and it is very likely other unanticipated expenses will come up. We can get a good idea of those expenses by looking at expenses over a long period of time.

Expenses are divided by your gross monthly income to get the debt-to-income ratio. Most mortgage companies want borrowers to have a .36 (or lower) debt-to-income ratio.

Debt-to-asset ratio is simply total liabilities divided by total assets. The higher the ratio, the greater leveraged the assets are. Debt-to-asset ratio is much more important for companies than it is for an individual. Nevertheless, it does come into play. It is the debt-to-asset ratio that leads a lender to require a 20% down payment on a home or a significant down payment on a car. You will want a working knowledge of debt-to-asset ratio when you start to invest. Obviously, the better the investment, the better your debt-to-asset ratio will be.

Some things you do to rebuild your credit are worthwhile and some are not. Simply stated, your credit score, debt-to-asset ratio and debt-to-income ratio are all important. Understand however, that one action may increase one factor and reduce another factor. You want to understand and maneuver all of the factors in order to optimize your credit. The higher the optimization, the lower credit costs you. An interest rate is what you pay for credit. Good credit is largely based on your ability to prove you can handle credit responsibly.

Your credit score is also important. It might be difficult to know where to start, but once you start, you will find that building a good credit score is simply a matter of following the plan you already put together. A credit score is largely, but not completely, an evaluation of your credit history. The first step is to monitor your score to make sure it is based on your history. It may seem obvious, but often credit scores are based on other people's history. Believe it or not, credit reporting agencies are not always right.

Clearly, judgments, charge-offs, late payments and other negative information have an adverse impact on your credit history. They may not, however, have the greatest impact. It is possible a mistake in the credit reporting records will have the greatest impact. You should look at your credit report to make sure the personal information on your credit reports is correct. Look for a misspelled name or an incorrect address where you've never lived. Both could indicate that your credit score is mixed up with somebody else's history. Take the seemingly minor errors seriously as they can have a negative impact on your credit report.

Remember, you have very little control over what has happened in the past but you have a great deal of control over what happens in the future. Nevertheless, you do have some control. Make sure to monitor your credit and ensure that negative reports go off when they should and that there are no errors on your report. The Fair Credit Reporting Act limits what a creditor can report.

One thing you can also do is to challenge previous credit scores. That is just about the only thing you can do to address your past credit history. Each credit reporting agency has their own rules for how to dispute errors on you report. There are also three main credit reporting agencies. Check all of them to make sure they are accurate. Contact the agency with the error to determine their process for a challenge. Each credit reporting agency has their own formal process that you will need to precisely follow. A phone call will not suffice with any of the main credit reporting agencies.

The last time I did one we were required to use their forms for one of the credit reporting agencies while another agency allowed us to craft our own letter, but it had to include specific information to be considered. The process may have changed since then and it may change again so it is important you obtain their written procedure and follow their precise rules. If you don't, they claim to have no obligation to act to correct your credit report. If you do, they contact the creditor who is required to provide proof the report is accurate. If that does not correct the issue it is time to seek the services of an attorney. Creditors can be punished pursuant to the Fair Credit Reporting Act for violations. If you don't feel like you can follow the precise procedure, consult an attorney to help with that process as well.

If you feel like you don't have control at this

point you need to go back to the planning stage and make adjustments to your plan.

The next step is really quite simple to understand but might be harder to implement. Start by following your plan. If you are finding it hard to follow maybe it is time to recruit help. Kind of like recovering alcoholics have a sponsor. Find a person, professional or otherwise, who will encourage you, monitor you, and give you pep talks. Sometimes it is hard to form new habits. If your plan involves debt settlement, that is what you need to implement first. If your plan involves a bankruptcy, then that is where you need to start. Regardless, follow the plan. After you have dealt with your debt, you need to shift to savings and rebuilding credit.

Responsible use of a credit card is an excellent way to rebuild credit. It should go without saying that you cannot be late on any future payments. If you find it is still impossible to make your debts maybe it is time to revisit your budget and maybe even time to adjust your lifestyle, so it does not exceed your income. This is important enough to say. DON'T be late on any of your financial obligations even if it means revisiting your budget.

Likely, poor credit for any reason such as debt settlement or bankruptcy may leave you without a credit card. I think it is unrealistic to expect anybody in our society to live without a credit card. I tell my clients to get a credit card even if it has to be a secured credit card ***unless*** they cannot control their impulses and would just charge it to its limit. If you have a plan to get out of debt without debt settlement or the filing a bankruptcy, just continue to follow your plan.

When you get to the point you can again use the credit card to charge and pay, do so wisely. If you filed a bankruptcy, apply for a new credit card as soon as the bankruptcy is complete. It might, however, be difficult to be approved for a credit card after bankruptcy. Maybe I should rephrase that. It will be easy getting a new credit card. You will have received many offers but those are the cards you want to avoid. Don't just jump into the first credit card you can get. Find a low interest credit card from a financial institution you trust.

Most financial advisors will advise you not to get a secured credit card because most of them don't report to credit bureaus. That is not entirely true. They don't generally report timely payments but if you are late in payments, they will make a negative credit report. Also, as you use the card responsibly, they will slowly raise your credit limit and begin to treat you just as they do all of their credit card customers and that includes making reports of timely payments. It is preferable to get a secured credit card than a credit card that has a high interest rate. Secured credit cards usually have a much lower interest rate.

The second secret about credit cards is that they don't make a report if you charge and pay off each month. I recommend that you always maintain a very low $10.00 balance. That way, most credit card companies will make a monthly report that you are current. Again, secured credit cards won't initially report your credit history if it is completely secured but as we discussed, secured credit cards will monitor your history and as you show the ability to stay current, they will slowly increase the credit limit and the card will no longer be fully secured. When that happens, they start to report your payment history. That is also a time when many people fall off their plan. They are enticed by the credit limit and start spending; DON'T start spending just because it is there.

I tell my clients that everybody buys groceries, and almost all grocery stores accept credit cards. Rather than writing out a check to the grocery store, charge the groceries and immediately write the check to the credit card company. I know, I'm old. Nobody uses checks anymore, but you get the point; make that payment immediately. Groceries provide the perfect time to use your credit cards within your budget and still have the ability to pay. Many financial advisors tell clients to go buy a vehicle, so you have a timely made monthly payment that is reported to the credit bureaus. That is good advice only if you need a car and only if it fits in your budget. Buying groceries and paying the credit card balance down each month is a better option. But remember, keep a very small balance. A balance where you pay very little interest but still trigger a credit report. It does not have to be a lot, a $10.00 balance will trigger a report and not accrue more than a few pennies a month in interest.

One or possibly two credit cards can help you rebuild your credit score. Maintain more credit cards and it starts to hurt your credit. A good debt to credit ratio is very important for each card you maintain your debt to credit ratio will include a minimum payment of about $10.00 for each card in your name even if they are paid off. That means if you have eight cards your debt to credit ratio takes an $80.00 hit.

There is really no reason you need more than one or two cards. The only reason is if you want to be able to monitor certain purchases. As I stated earlier, I like to buy Venti Chai with Almond Milk from Starbucks. My wife pointed out I was spending a lot of money each month at Starbucks.

Frankly, I was not taking my own advice and was letting my Starbucks spending control me rather than me controlling my Starbucks spending. I started using one credit card for Starbucks and nothing else and that is when I noticed how much I was spending. That is also when we reevaluated our budget and decided Starbucks once a week was enough.

If you currently have 10 credit cards, pay them off pursuant to the plan you have for getting out of debt and then cancel most of them. Don't start using any others until the last one is paid off. The exception is for groceries as we discussed.

If you are unable to put together a plan that will allow you to pay off your debts in a reasonable amount of time, you need to consider another option. Don't make that decision on your own. Talk to an attorney or some other qualified professional who can give you guidance and help you evaluate and recommend a course of action that is in your best interest. This is the time when an attorney may not be the best person for the job unless you also need to resolve a debt crisis at the same time.

Recap:

1. Evaluate your credit worthiness
    a. Credit Score
    b. Debt-to-Income ratio
    c. Debt-to-Asset ratio
2. Gain or regain control
3. Use Credit Cards Wisely

Conclusion

The most important thing you can remember is that you can do this. Follow the steps outlined in each section and you will be able to build a healthy financial future. There will be bumps in the road. Your goal is to get into a financial position where you can handle the bumps.

The alternative is to keep doing what you have always done and continue to have your finances drive you rather than you driving your finances. If you do the driving, you will find that you have a lot less anxiety in your life. Planning is the opposite of worrying. Worrying accomplishes nothing. It doesn't help, it only gives you anxiety so stop worrying and start making a plan.

Peace is very important. Hopefully, the things you have learned in this book will allow you a lot of peace each day as you make and follow your financial plan. Pablo Picasso said it perfectly:

> *Our goals can only be reached through a vehicle of a plan, in which we must fervently*

believe, and upon which we must vigorously act. There is no other route to success

.

Hopefully, this book will help you put together a well thought out plan that you fervently believe in and that you have found the tools you need to act on the plan. If you do so, you will achieve the success you desire and deserve.

Made in the USA
Monee, IL
04 November 2026

67380057R00095